In Praise of *Riding the Rocket*

This book lives up to its title and gives you answers that really help you!

Riding the Rocket: How to Manage your Modern Career has been written to be used and provides us with useful thoughts and insights about being a success, changing careers and looking after ourselves at work.

The chapter about using our intuition to choose a job that we are well suited for was really inspiring. A novel and useful way of helping us to decide on a career path! We can also make a positive choice to learn from our past, be in charge and make our modern career what we want it to be. A great book!

Angela Farmer, General Manager, Guys Dental Hospital

This is a great book for anyone who is working – no matter what stage of your career you might be at. Packed full of practical advice, top tips and some truly hands-on life lessons, *Riding the Rocket* is an insightful read.

I particularly love Richard's 'Antidotes' – he has converted me from a life-long 'Ignorer' to a 'Chooser'.

Anna Stevenson, Director, Stevenson Consulting

Sometimes it takes a major life event to make you stop and think; is this really what life and work are all about? *Riding the Rocket* is a book that not only helps you take stock of who you are and what you have achieved, but helps guide you on your future path and frame some choices at your own pace.

To make the best use of this book, make yourself a delicious cheese sandwich (Richard does mention sandwiches), sit down and work through the exercises and see where your own rocket ride takes you. Life is often not easy and with this book in our pocket, we can make it much easier for ourselves.

Erin Weston, Human Resources and Occupational Health and Safety Coordinator, Brophy Family and Youth Services, Warrnambool, Australia

Riding the Rocket brings together a valuable and potent mix of intuition, evidence and experienced views to help you on your rocket – probably more than any of us, either individually or with a group of well-meaning friends, can pull together.

Richard has included useful tools and thought-provoking exercises that you can use for your rocket. Reading this book is like having a lovely coaching session – you just need to add you to the mix. Good luck!

Andie Hallihan, Director, Applied Angle

Richard's *Riding the Rocket* holds a full cargo of instruments, tools and techniques to help us actively manage our career. Trajectories don't necessarily go straight up in a predictable pattern and his skilfully crafted work helps to align, direct and manage our career in a path of our choosing – and it's good to know that we do have some choice, no matter how off course our flight pattern might feel at times!

An enjoyable read with lots of practical tools, to create an enjoyable future!

Helen Fisher, Business Consultant

We all know that we are in times of constant change, so our ability to manage this change and make good career decisions is essential. This book hits the mark and is a valuable addition to the series. Looking after our 'career engine' and ensuring we keep powering along will reap benefits for all.

The toolkit and companion e-book (*Building the Rocket*) are both excellent and full of practical tips.

Kevin Bennett, Director, KB Business Solutions Pty Ltd, Australia

RIDING THE ROCKET

RICHARD MAUN

RIDING
THE ROCKET

How to manage your modern career

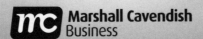

Marshall Cavendish Business

Published in 2013 by Marshall Cavendish Business
An imprint of Marshall Cavendish International

1 New Industrial Road, Singapore 536196
genrefsales@marshallcavendish.com
www.marshallcavendish.com/genref

Other Marshall Cavendish offices: Marshall Cavendish Corporation, 99 White Plains Road, Tarrytown, NY 10591 • Marshall Cavendish International (Thailand) Co Ltd. 253 Asoke, 12th Flr, Sukhumvit 21 Road, Klongtoey Nua, Wattana, Bangkok 10110, Thailand • Marshall Cavendish (Malaysia) Sdn Bhd, Times Subang, Lot 46, Subang Hi-Tech Industrial Park, Batu Tiga, 40000 Shah Alam, Selangor Darul Ehsan, Malaysia

Marshall Cavendish is a trademark of Times Publishing Limited

A CIP record for this book is available from the British Library

ISBN 978 981 4408 28 8

Printed and bound in Great Britain by TJ International Limited, Padstow, Cornwall

DISCLAIMER

Please note: This book is full of real life examples and stories. However, personal details have all been changed to preserve anonymity, so if you think you know whom I was writing about you are mistaken. It was someone else completely, from a different place and a different time, riding a different rocket.

For Steve and Graham

For their support and generosity.

CONTENTS

We live in the age of the modern career, where we have to fend for ourselves and be proactive to ensure we have a happy, successful and rewarding life. We do this by riding the rocket through the arc of our career, from our first working day to our last. Our rocket transports us through space and time and we decide how high to fly, how fast we travel and where we go – we're in control.

This book is intended to support us on our journey and to provide essential insights and tools to enable us to keep safe, make good decisions and create opportunities for development and career change.

Please read the detailed contents and ask yourself:
- How can I use this book to help me make progress?
- What aspect of my career needs attention?
- Which item do I need to read now?

3. FRAMING OUR CAREER – Progress To Date

4. MODERN CAREER THINKING – Key Skills For Success

5. AWARENESS PLEASE – Don't Be A Tourist

6. HOW TO CHOOSE CAREERS – Navigation Lessons

7. SETTING CAREER GOALS – Money vs. Happiness

8. HOW TO CHANGE CAREERS – Pulling G

9. CAREER ACCELERATORS – Flying Higher, Flying Faster

10. THE CAREER KILLERS – Becoming Toxic

11. AN ESSENTIAL GUIDE TO CAREER TRENDS – Preparing For The Future

12. LONGEVITY – Waving Goodbye

13. TAKE THE CONTROLS – Put The Learning Into Practice

14. TOOLKIT – One Life, One Rocket

PREVIEW OF *BUILDING THE ROCKET* – Companion Mini E-book

INTRODUCING OTHER RICHARD MAUN BOOKS FROM MARSHALL CAVENDISH   249

Bouncing Back
How To Keep Your Job
Job Hunting 3.0
Leave The B@$T@RDS Behind
My Boss Is A Bastard

Preface

TIME TO FLY!

Forget what you know about careers, because the traditional 'career ladder' approach of steady increments and long service is rapidly being consigned to history. In its place we have the *modern career* – a composite of roles and industries, contracts, self-employment, consultancy, changes, risks and rewards. We need to be proactive, take responsibility for our own training and development, be aware of our strengths and how we respond under pressure and plan ahead for the future. A modern career means having a modern attitude and to achieve that we need to remember:

We have one key task – *riding the rocket*.

A 'career' is the span of our working lives and by riding the rocket we take responsibility for the speed, height, course and destination of our career. We need to tighten the straps of our seat in the nose cone, calibrate the gauges, take a firm hold of the control column, fire up the engines and throttle up. It's not always going to be a smooth ride and it may be scary at times, yet riding the rocket and being in control is both exhilarating and rewarding – and essential.

We fly our rocket over the terrain of the marketplace we inhabit and we can choose to stay on the same flight path, cruising low enough to enjoy the view and skim mountain tops. We can also zoom up into the stratosphere, push the boost button and journey through space to a new planet, a new marketplace and a change of career.

Eventually we will have to slow down and think about returning to the ground and how and where we want to land our rocket. Should we park it permanently in the hanger, or perhaps give it a rest and maybe only take it for occasional 'short flights'?

It's our life and our career – and it's our rocket. We're in control and even if we get buffeted by solar winds, lashed by thunderstorms and are forced to change direction, we can always create new opportunities for ourselves, take time to think and then decide what we want to do next.

Like it or not, we're strapped in for the ride of our lives. However, we now have this book to help guide us, to inform our thinking and to remind us that we're normal people who can make mistakes, learn new things and get on with our lives. With this book next to us in the locker, we have a flight manual to guide us when we need practical support.

UNIQUE CONTENT

Riding the Rocket has been written to enable us all to successfully manage our modern career and the contents have been drawn from real life success stories, good practice, useful tools and clear thinking. The book is set up to make it easy to dip into, so that you can read the sections that have the most value for you. The contents include:

- How to choose careers.
- How to change careers.
- How to accelerate our career.
- How to avoid killing our career.
- An essential guide to career trends.
- Practical toolkit.

Each chapter features tools and tips, models, questions and case studies. There is also a handy summary section at the end of the book to remind us of the essential tools and to make it easy to find something useful when we're in a hurry.

UNIQUE COMBINATIONS ADD VALUE

In writing this book, I've revisited my extensive practical experience as a careers coach, a senior operations manager, a best-selling careers writer, an executive development specialist, a leadership and communication skills lecturer, a process improvement professional, a business radio show host and a creative thinker. I have collected many work-related hats over the years and have successfully shifted my own career to take advantage of new opportunities and to learn new skills. Unique combinations add value because they create something special. I love that I've had a varied career – I always enjoy combining experience and practical insights with process improvement thinking and psycho-dynamic approaches. It's great fun to work with talented people and to support them on their journeys as they make sense of disasters, achieve promotions and make significant career changes.

While the case studies in the book are all based on real people and real events, they have all been carefully anonymised to protect the guilty and spare the blushes of the innocent, because we're all allowed to make mistakes, be brilliant and find a path that works for us.

OUR KEY DEVELOPMENTAL TASK

In any development situation there is often one thing which stands apart from the others and grabs our attention – this is our key development task. When I worked with a mentor many years ago I was struggling to fit my ambition to my maturity, in my haste to become a senior manager, and I asked him what he thought my key development task was. Without hesitation, he fixed me with a twinkling eye and said:

'Richard, you need to develop gravitas.'

It took me a while, but once I worked out exactly how to achieve that, I began to do better when getting my point across and being listened to. However, on some days I'm sure I forget to pack my gravitas in my briefcase and it teaches me that I still have something left to learn. That's my story, so what's yours? What's your key developmental task that will help you to successfully ride the rocket? The answer is likely to be lurking within these chapters, so please think about it as you read on.

YOU CAN CHOOSE

Before we let you loose with your own rocket, let's be clear that all decisions and indecisions, actions and inactions that you take after reading this book are *your own responsibility*. You are your own person, complete with skills and talents, fears and phobias, dreams and ambitions. We all have a right to a happy life and we all have to work hard to make that a reality. However, this is now *your* book to read and *your* life to live – so you're free to choose the bits of the book that work best for you and to enjoy exploring your world.

ACKNOWLEDGEMENTS

Although writing is often a lonely sport, it's impossible to work in total isolation and I'm fortunate enough to know generous, warm hearted, witty people, who lend a hand when asked and prevent me from succumbing to cabin fever. This book has been written with love and supported by all of these splendid people:

1) Firstly, I need to thank the team at Marshall Cavendish who worked hard to breathe life into my manuscript and turn it into a finished book. Hearty thanks go to Violet Phoon for publishing this book, Melvin Neo, Stephanie Yeo and Janine Gamilla for organising the contents, cover and marketing,

and also the editors and designers who smoothed the text and polished the artwork. Thank you all!

2) Secondly, I offer my heartfelt thanks to the group of busy professionals who contributed their ideas and stories that form the backbone of the chapter about future trends. I assembled a team of international senior managers, consultants, recruiters and clear thinkers and invited them to share their insights. Looking into the future is always risky when we do so alone, but enlist another 16 pairs of eyes and the outlook has more depth and colour to it. I'm extremely grateful to the following people for their brilliant contribution: Jim Banting, Cecily Barber, Kevin Bennett, Gavin Drake, Iain Duckworth, Jordan Dudley, Helen Fisher, Sara Greenfield, Kerri-Ann Hargreaves, Katrin Klüber, Claire Lancaster, Justin Paul, Kimberley Plumley, Meg Pringle, Anna Stevenson, Victoria Tomlinson and Graham Townsend.

3) Thirdly, I'd like to thank Julie Bishop for her insights, enthusiasm and brilliant co-hosting of our weekly business show on Future Radio. We've spent 18 months meeting people from all walks of life and it's been amazing to learn about how they have developed their careers. All of that experience has percolated into this book too, so thank you Julie.

4) The fourth group is my trusty team of readers, supporters and people who share their energy with me so that I can keep writing when the days are long and the nights are short. Love and appreciation goes to Steve Tracey, Julie Holmes, Helen Fisher, Katrin Klüber, Graham Townsend and Ria Varnom,

who have come along for the ride and provided support when I needed it.

5) The fifth and final group are five people who give me the space and time to write, which is amazingly generous of them. Without them around, life would be very dull and it's great to stop work and smile when they bring me tea to drink, cake to eat and cuddly toys to keep me company. All my love goes to Rebecca and our four noisy, lovely, brilliant children – Lucy, Theodore, Oscar and Harvey.

Thank you everyone, I'm blessed to have you all in my life.

Richard Maun
Norfolk
England

For coaching, training courses, public speaking and e-publishing, visit **www.richardmaun.com**

Richard can also be contacted via:
Modern Careers Blog: www.richardmaun.com/writing
Facebook Page: Richard Maun – Modern Careers
LinkedIn: Richard Maun
Twitter: @RichardMaun
Skype: richardmaun

1
Careers Count
– Riding Our Rocket –

COCKPIT QUESTION:
What does it feel like to be strapped into a rocket?

START HERE

This is important. Whatever our thoughts are when we hear the word 'career', the key thing to remember is that it is an essential concept. A career outlines the arc of our working life and creates the opportunity for us to manage our progress, instead of just bouncing through life like a ball bearing in a pinball machine. It doesn't matter what sort of work we do – whether we are a professional manager, a skilled craft worker, an ingenious technician or a polite service worker, we all have a career and owe it to ourselves to take care of ourselves. We need to make sure we have the skills and support to continue our life in a way that satisfies us. It doesn't matter how old we are or how far we are through our working life, it's always worth pausing to reflect on the concept of 'our career' and think about where we are now and what is in store for us over the remainder of our working life.

A CAREER... is how we spend our time
between starting work and retiring.

A CAREER... encompasses our dreams and our ambitions
and the things we do to make them a reality.

A CAREER... is the content of our working life and
includes all periods of work, job hunting and
vocational training and development.

This means that we all have a career and that this book has relevance to all of us, whatever our life's path has presented us with.

USE THIS BOOK

Riding the Rocket has been written to be used. It's based on first-hand stories of success and failure and contains practical tools and concepts to help us think, plan and do. If we don't *think*, our decisions could be hasty or risky. If we don't *plan* then at some point we could end up in the middle of nowhere and find our rocket buried in the sand, having run out of fuel and crashed. And of course if we don't do *anything* then it's just an exercise in navel gazing and fantastical thinking. Therefore, we can use this book to guide us, to reassure us and to promote better decision making, because that's at the heart of a successful career of any sort.

FORGET SCHOOL

For many of us, the word 'career' is synonymous with a bored teacher in a scruffy office surrounded by uninspiring leaflets. People talk about how they loved studying history at school, or literature, or science, but they never wax lyrical about happy hours spent in the careers office, eagerly reading up on a wide variety of jobs and professions. Talking about careers is not glamorous, it's not the sexy go-to subject at university, in the same way that people introducing themselves as an accountant at a dinner party are likely to be greeted with a polite nod of interest and a bored enquiry along the lines of 'that's nice, have you always wanted to add up columns of numbers?'[1]

It's amazing that the four big aspects of our life – work, marriage (or partnership), parenthood and household management – are not mandatory secondary school qualifications. Knowing what the Aztecs did is quite interesting, as is the correct pronunciation of Popocatepetl, but such information is useless when trying to balance the monthly household expenses or going five rounds with a bank manager who is determined to sell us an inappropriately expensive mortgage, without explaining why we need their pension package as part of the deal. It's no wonder that people find the world a bewildering place, when the training for our part in it is 80% about passing exams and 20% about physical education on a wet Wednesday.

Given that we also spend a large amount of time at school worrying about kittens, fashion, how to kiss and whether our team is going to win the league this year, it's not surprising that

[1] Accounting is a useful and noble profession. However, having started out as a trainee accountant, I can testify that it never set the dinner party conversation alight when I was introduced as such.

most people give the careers office a wide berth. It feels safer to concentrate on passing our exams and to spend energy growing taller and so we tend to kick the idea of 'work' into the long grass for the time being. And then we wake up in our 30s or 40s and think 'Hang on! How did I get here? What am I doing with my life?' At this point it suddenly matters to think about a career and we wish we had paid more attention to books like this when we were younger.

So, forget school and any negative preconceptions you might have about the word 'career'. You were misinformed, badly led or just too young and immature to properly comprehend what a wonderful, useful and absolutely *essential* concept it is.

THE MODERN CAREER IS HERE

In this book we will keep encountering the words 'modern career' – the next chapter will go into the concept in more detail. There is also a chapter about modern careers in the book *Bouncing Back*, which was written to help people get started again after a career setback.

The reason for coining the term 'modern career' is that the world has shifted markedly over the last 20 years. Instead of a career ladder of long service for a loyal organisation, resulting in a steady climb from post-room clerk to chairman (or woman) of the board and regular pay rises along the way, we now have something much trickier to work with. Organisations can be loyal, but they often get buffeted by global tax regimes, competition and the latest consumer trend, which results in them having to move staff or reinvent themselves entirely, necessitating redundancies and large-scale personnel changes.

A later chapter looks at the six Career Challenges we face in working our way through our modern career. For now, we just need to accept the central theme to this book – *we are responsible for our working life and need to manage ourselves for the duration of it*. The world doesn't owe us a favour and it will not come knocking on our door, so we need to be thoughtful and resourceful, keep ourselves in awareness and remain proactive throughout our working life.

RICKETY ROCKET?

We are sitting in the cockpit of our rocket, strapped in with our helmet on and watching our life flash past the windows at a frightening pace. The dials and displays tell us what direction we're heading in, our height and speed and the amount of fuel we have left. There's no autopilot in here though, no clever little system to keep things on track for us while we take a nap. If we take our eyes off the dials or relax our grip on the control column, we could veer off course, pull up sharply and stall, or lose sight of the horizon and fall to earth nose down. We don't want to be in a rickety rocket either, we need to be in one that is properly screwed together and doesn't have bits falling off – it needs to be a tidy, well maintained piece of equipment. In practice, this means we need to understand ourselves so that we focus our energy productively and not ride in a third-rate rickety rocket of ignorance.

We are in the cockpit alone. We can radio out for help and support of course, but we are the only person to see the world in our own unique way – we filter out unhelpful pieces of information, fantasise about what the reality might be and construct an existence that makes sense to us and keeps us safe.

As a result of all this we need to accept that however clever we think we might be, the chances are that we are missing vital bits of information and are gently skewing the world to fit our needs at the time, which can lead to disastrous results. We might miss our impending redundancy, overlook the end of preferential business tax rates which can mean our organisation is about to decamp to the next best tax zone, or simply ignore the fact that our daily work rate has declined to the point where our line manager is wondering if we'd be more useful as a hat stand.

Whether we like it or not, we are all sitting in the control centre of our own career-rocket that is shooting us through time from school to retirement. Our responsibility is to grip the controls, read the dials, take note of the information readouts and make sure we are in charge.

We're riding the rocket through our entire life.

Like it. Hate it. But don't ever ignore it.

SO WHAT?

This is all well and good, we accept that the world can be an ugly place and that if we don't take control our career could spiral out of orbit and suddenly we're in charge of a husband (or wife) and two children with no income and in a profession that no longer needs us. The challenge is for us to accept that we can have a happier, more fulfilling life if we choose to ride the rocket *with our eyes open*. If we're reading this while employed then we're already inside the rocket (or maybe hanging on grimly if yours is one of those old-fashioned open-air models) – so the choice we face isn't whether to ride it or not, it's to decide to consciously be the one in charge.

What is needed for success is to tap into *uncommon sense* and make it work for us. Consider this chart below and ask yourself which group you fall into and which one you will stay in after you've read this book (given that you *are* reading this book, then it's obvious you'll be in either D or E).

RICHARD'S 'BE UNCOMMON' GROUP CLASSIFICATION

GROUP A IGNORERS	GROUP B LEAVERS	GROUP C DISMISSERS	GROUP D ACCEPTERS	GROUP E CHOOSERS
Those who don't buy career books, because they're dull.	Those who buy career books because they feel it's the right thing to do, but then leave them on the shelf to sweat their way into their brain.	Those who actually read the books they buy, but tend to cough and crow that they're full of common sense and add little value	Those who are big enough to realise that such books do contain genuinely useful ideas to support increased success.	Those who buy the books, read the books, choose ideas and tools that appeal to them and then actually put them into practice.

GROUP A IGNORERS	GROUP B LEAVERS	GROUP C DISMISSERS	GROUP D ACCEPTERS	GROUP E CHOOSERS
No progress is made	No progress is made	No progress is made	Some progress is made	Reasonable, sustained progress is made. If you're here then you're really uncommon and can celebrate!

In my experience as a coach and a lecturer, the majority of the population tend to be Ignorers, Leavers or Dismissers. They feel they know better, or perhaps are just too intimidated by life to admit their weaknesses and find support. The minority of the population fall into the Accepters and Choosers groups – which is why it's *uncommon* sense and rarer than you might think for people to choose to ride the rocket. For example, how many people do you know own a book about successful job hunting and a book about career management and spend one day a year re-reading them and taking stock?

When we think about the 'so what?' question the answer becomes obvious – by consciously riding the rocket we gain a competitive workplace advantage over the majority of our peers. It's a simple as that.

We're riding the rocket and we're brilliant at it.

LEARNING EXERCISE

As we're going to spend the rest of the book talking about rockets, we may as well have one in our mind. For fun, please use this space below to draw your own rocket. What size is it relative to the landscape? Is it pointing up or down? Can you see yourself peering out of the cockpit window?

2
The Career Engine
– Keeping Us In Flight –

COCKPIT QUESTION:
Which influencers do we need to ignore, and which ones do we need to listen to?

NO POWER, NO GO

This book will help us to have a fulfilling modern career and enjoy ourselves as we ride our rocket with its various controls and gauges, levers and exciting buttons. We get to try them all and we have complete control over our rocket.

The idea of hurtling along at speed in a sleek rocket might be both exhilarating and a little scary, but there's nothing wrong in having both of these feelings. It's similar to being at an adventure park and finding ourselves at the head of the queue for the latest ride called The Cosmic Plunge of Almost Certain Death!

These amusement rides tease us with their scary names and information about how much time we will spend defying gravity when we ride them. They're fun and frightening and after we've experienced the requisite 90 seconds of blind terror and jaw-dropping exhilaration, we limp away smiling and badgering our friends to queue up for second turn. If you want to simulate your career in one 90-second burst, head to your nearest amusement park and choose the biggest, ugliest, fastest ride there is and strap yourself in tight.

Once you step off, grinning wildly at the people waiting in the queue to reassure them that it really *is* that scary, stop and notice how the ride is powered, because without power there is no ride, just a collection of cars and tracks.

THE CAREER ENGINE

Roller-coasters, rockets and careers all need power – they all have engines as a core part of their design. So before we go into detail about various aspects of how we can manage our career, we need to pay attention to the power pack that's keeping us in the air – *our career engine*.

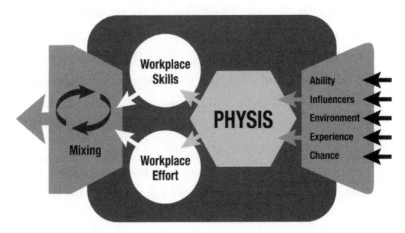

The word *physis* is a new word for us to get to know, and not a misspelling. Please read on and all will be explained.

Jet engines operate on the *suck – squeeze – bang – blow* principle. Air is drawn in and mixed with fuel vapour, which is compressed and then ignited to produce a controlled explosion. This creates a stream of superheated gas, which pushes out through the exhaust system, causing the forward motion of the engine and the airframe it is attached to.

Our career rocket has a unique engine that works along similar lines:

1. **Suck.** We suck in experience of life and work, are influenced by people around us, have latent ability, respond to our environment and are open to the whim of random events.

2. **Squeeze.** These forces and elements meet our internal sense of *physis*, our life force, which processes them and 'decides' whether to acknowledge them or reject them, and to what degree.

3. **Bang.** Being a wellspring of energy and choice, our physis then powers the application of workplace skills and the amount of effort to be used deploying them.

4. **Blow.** These skills and effort mix to produce outcomes, which provide the raw thrust to our engine every day. This in turn propels our rocket forward and through the arc of our career.

Having seen the engine in its complete form, we will now strip it down to its component parts and consider each one in turn, starting with perhaps the most important concept that you've probably never heard of until a moment ago – *physis*.

1. PHYSIS

The word physis means *life force*. We all have a life force inside us that is part of what makes us who we are. The concept dates back to antiquity and in ancient Greek the word physis meant 'nature'. Physis is a concept that describes the force that keeps us pushing forward, gets us up in the morning and keeps us working late into the night. It's the force that enables us to be ambitious and to achieve challenging goals, devote energy to learning new skills and powers us through tough times.

The word *physics* is derived from the word *physis* and is the study of how things move through time and space in the natural world. It's important to emphasise that physis is just a concept – we can't see it or touch it, it's simply a helpful word to describe the force of life inside us.[2]

In nature, physis is used to describe the force that allows a seed to develop and push up shoots through packed earth, or go around a paving slab. A seed is one of the smallest packets of energy in the natural world and when a seed releases that energy and continues to absorb nutrients and convert it to further growth, it turns from a tiny speck to a tall sunflower, or a stout oak tree. We too can become healthy, strong oak trees.

In terms of our careers, it is physis that makes our decisions and our choices *ours*, which means that:

- We cannot blame others for our current predicament –

[2]   There is an entire chapter about Physis in my book *Bouncing Back*. The chapter looks at how we can get physis to flow and relates it to the process of transition as we confront a career issue and then engage our energy to make progress in resolving it.

we have the power to say 'no thank you' or 'not in this way'.

- We have the inbuilt drive to achieve difficult targets and reach high goals.
- We can take care of ourselves so that we can continue to ride the rocket and not burn out our engine through over-stressed activity.

We are our own person and not mini versions of our parents, guardians or school teachers.

Physis is part of what makes us all unique, special and talented. If we follow a career that we're interested in and motivated to do well at then we'll open the metaphorical 'sluice gates' inside us, enabling physis to flow at a greater rate, helping to power us forward. Conversely, if we spend our lives trudging through a dull job as part of an unfulfilling career then we shut the sluice gate and only let a trickle of the potential flow through. We choose our own career, which is why it's so important that we follow our hearts (or get as close to it as we can) when selecting jobs and building a career path.

Physis is the force that lets us listen to our parents while making up our own minds. It's the force that keeps us in the library researching a subject we're interested in. It's the force that filters all the inputs to our engine. In practice, this means that we can work in a poor environment and still find the energy to have a great time. We can be born into a world with poor life choices and can still graduate from a top university and we can keep our rocket flying through storm clouds and high winds in our career.

As the truism has it: 'Do a job you love and you'll never have to work for a day.' We can all engage our physis to enable us to achieve that outcome and we're all skilful enough to make that happen, if we want it to.

2. ABILITY

This relates to the natural talents that we're born with. We might have an eye for art, be quick with arithmetic, spot patterns in the landscape, understand the central theme in a work of literature, absorb other languages, ask intelligent questions about science, or have a ready smile and a warm way with people.

Knowing what we're good at means we can put more useful abilities to work in our engine. If we focus on using our strengths we leave ourselves with capacity to grow and we are more likely to excel in a competitive environment. There is a section on ability in the later chapter about choosing a career.

3. INFLUENCERS

There are three key groups of people who attempt to shape our thinking, sometimes by encouraging us to think more broadly, other times by ignoring facts and following their own unsavoury logic. These three groups are:

- **Parents.** This means any person who helped to raise us. Our parental figures gave us permission to act, based on our observations of their behaviour when we were young children. They may have tried to exhort us to achieve demanding targets, or curtailed our ambition with an ignorant 'we don't do things like that in our family'.

- **Peers.** Our peer group made a significant difference to our performance at school. People like to fit in with their tribe and if ours was one that valued good work and high marks, then we're more likely to have achieved them as well. In our adult life our peer group can either support us or hold us back and a career change is often made easier by making new friends and finding new people to support us on our journey.

- **Powers.** The powers are the other influential people in our lives who orbit around us. These could be an uncle who we look up to, our first line manager who taught us how to manage at work, or our life partner who encourages us to go out into the world and reach for ambitions. These people carry weight because they are powerful to us. That doesn't always make them right and it's useful to bear in mind that in many cases, the powerful person has a plan of their own and their advice to us could be based on helping them achieve that plan.

All of these groups may have meant well, or been recycling second-hand bits of wisdom or clinging to unhelpful stereotypes. It's up to us to decide which bits we accept and which we discard.

4. ENVIRONMENT

This is the physical world we inhabit. The sunlight we feel on our face, the comfort of our chair, the forbiddingly gloomy reception desk, the battleship grey office, or the brightly lit shared zone with hot-desks and a busy coffee shop. Our environment also includes the uniform we wear and the codes we conform to. If we work in a grey, lifeless office then it's likely that we will find ourselves uninspired and keen to escape. If we work in a noisy office we may prefer to find a job that allows us to work from home. I know that I used to thoroughly resent having to wear a suit and drive to an office to write reports that I could have produced at home without any of the inconvenience driving to work entails. As a result, one of the key factors for me to change my career was the freedom to act and to choose the environment I worked in.

CAREER TOP TIP

*The more autonomy we have over our working day,
the less stressed we tend to be.*

We can prize autonomy and the flexibility to choose as
two of the most important facets of a successful and
happy modern career.

---

5. EXPERIENCE

If we enjoy learning through doing things, we value our experiences very highly because they inform our thinking. Experience also enables us to weigh our options and to sharpen our senses so we can make good choices. However, if our rocket is powering us forward across an uncharted landscape, we may not have any experiences to aid in our decision making. This can reduce the efficiency of our engine as we struggle to work out what to do.

When this happens we need to call on the experience of other people, either by talking with a colleague, interviewing support staff or seeking impartial knowledge from a trusted mentor. This experience lag tends to happen in the first 30 days of a new job, when we often wonder what made us take the role and we lie awake at night worrying about it. It also happens when we first get promoted to a leadership position, because no matter how much leadership training we have completed it is almost impossible to experience being one without actually being in the role. It suggests that when we do get promoted we need to be first in the queue for coaching support to help us make the transition from follower to leader.

6. CHANCE

Although it is said that 'you make your own luck', it is also true that there are times when you can't control the wind; you simply have to ride the storm as best you can. Our engine sucks in chance events that can lead to new and exciting challenges or to the door being slammed behind us. Personally, I subscribe to the following outlook and often pose the same question to colleagues, resulting in us coming up with new products and new working agreements, instead of sulking that we've been dealt a bad hand. My outlook is:

> **ALWAYS ASK:**
> What's the opportunity?

Putting this another way, people like to quote the aphorism 'if life hands you lemons, then make lemonade'. I prefer my colleague Ria's take on it:

> 'If life hands you lemons and you don't want lemonade, put them down, go and find oranges and make orangeade instead.'

This also links back to our *Influencers* because they tend to leave us with such sayings, which shape our response to chance and opportunity. New words mean new outcomes and we can all make orangeade if we choose to.

7. WORKPLACE SKILLS

Our physis engages with the various inputs described above and we head off in a particular direction. In rocket engine terms, this means that we tend to use some, but not all, of our workplace skills. The truth is that we just have 'skills' and there is a great overlap between our work life and home life. For example, when I'm teaching people communication skills I always invite them to practice positive approaches at home with their partner or their children. It makes perfect sense to me to practice this kind of skill as much as possible so that when we come to work and really need it, we already have a well-developed repertoire.

Ask yourself:

- Which skills do I always use?
- Which skills did I make good use of before and have forgotten about along the way?

Successful people engage all their strengths and delegate their weaknesses. We can do that too.

8. WORKPLACE EFFORT

Skills alone will not give us a great career. We need to apply them, which is why the practical application of skills and sustained effort mix to produce the vortex of energy that thrusts our rocket forward. Our physis will helpfully supply enough life force to sustain our effort, unless we've filled the intake with unhelpful influences and are grumbling at our poor environment and run of bad luck.

We need to be consistent and avoid a stop-go style that confuses people. We can work at a fast pace and then slow for a while, but we want to resist either running flat-out for sustained periods, or continually switching the engine off and on again. Choose a career that you like and which fits your energy patterns, so if you like to get out of the office consider a travelling sales job, for example. If you like to work late, then talk to your line manager about how you might work a more flexible pattern that better fits your style.

While this may seem a distant dream to many people, the number of workers taking time out to work at home is steadily increasing, and if we don't ask, we don't get. We'll talk more about these trends in the chapter about the future of working life.

9. MIXING

The skills we choose to deploy and the energy we put into the time we spend working, or looking for a job, or chasing down our next promotion are the superheated gases that propel us forward. All the other factors influence them and it's up to us to make sure we have a steady jet stream exiting the exhaust pipes of our rocket engine.

10. THRUST

We need thrust to stay in the air. Dial in too much and we will struggle to hang on the control column as the career G-forces pin us back in our seat. Conversely, if we aim for too little thrust, we will either have to accept flying at a lower altitude in a less satisfying post, or we may fail to clear the pinnacle of the next mountain and will tear a hole in our rocket.

Take a moment to think :
- Are you happy with your current altitude and speed?
- If not, what would you like to change?
- What is the first tiny step you could take to improve your situation?

BURN OUT

People who set their throttle to maximum power run the risk of 'running hot' when the engine works too hard and begins to creak and strain under the pressure of continually being pushed beyond a reasonable limit of tolerance. When this happens the engine is liable to seize up or break apart, not because we have suddenly run out of physis, but because the connections aren't working in the way that they need to. Our internal safety valve kicks in and we shut down, causing our rocket to fall out of the sky and land, perhaps with a gentle bump, but more likely with a harsh tearing of metal as we hit the ground and gouge a furrow in the soft earth.

For the moment our career has stalled and our engine is dead. We need to repair it and retune it, so that we can launch back up into the sky and get on our way.

SYSTEM MAINTENANCE

The rest of this book is, in essence, about maintaining our engine, because so much of how we live our working lives feeds into it, in the same way as the food we eat fuels our body and determines how healthy we might be. The best way to take care of our career engine is to:

> **HOW TO TAKE CARE OF OUR CAREER ENGINE**
> Quit smoking.
> Get more sleep.
> Drink less caffeine.
> Take time to stop and think.
> Walk 10,000 steps each day.
> Eat fresh fruit and vegetables.
> See a doctor when we're unwell.
> Take all of our holiday entitlement.
> Reduce stress by having control over how we do our work.
> Set aside at least two hours each weekend for leisure, away from work and our buzzing smartphone.

SO WHAT?

Without a decent power source we are going to scrape the ground or go nowhere. As we think about the work we currently do, the direction we would like to go in, our ability to remain aware of our surroundings and so on, we can use the idea of our career engine to keep asking ourselves:

- Are we helping the power to flow or are we choking off the output?

We don't have to be super clever to make sure our engine is well maintained and running effectively – we can simply keep in mind the things that have an impact and limit us. Perhaps we have a 'friend' who tends to have a gloomy view of life, or we believe the saying 'you've made your bed, now you've got to lay in it'.

The truth is, it's just a bed – we can change the duvet cover or find a new bed. We don't have to accept the status quo. Our engine is there working for us and is able to power us through this phase and across the landscape to somewhere new and more fulfilling.

LEARNING EXERCISE

The engine is a metaphor for the way we filter and absorb influences, process them and make both conscious and subconscious decisions about what to do. What is one thing that has stayed in your mind after reading this chapter? Take a moment to reflect and then write it here:

_____

_____

_____

3
Framing Our Career
– Progress To Date –

FRAMING COUNTS

When you frame a picture it can enhance it and add lustre, or it can spoil it and make it look a mess. Either way, the framing sets up responses inside us that cause us to make decisions – do we keep the picture? Move it? Get rid of it?

It's the same with careers – we frame our career in the way we tell people about it, whether we acknowledge the truth of where we are, or if we gloss over some troubling aspects of it. We tend to be creatures of habit and will often describe our career in the same way. This helps to us reinforce the position we're in and the danger is that we do nothing to change that position because we've grown accustomed to the situation and have forgotten how to make changes.

RICHARD'S STORY – A RUBBISH CAREER?

I always used to frame my career by telling people that I'd had a rubbish career so far. Was that the truth though, or was I overly focussed on negative aspects?

I have been made redundant four times and sacked once. To be fair, the sacking was because I had only been there six months and so was only entitled to a handshake and a cheery 'good riddance'. In this particular role I had been hired to improve the production process and had failed to spot the two owners bickering with each other during my interview. My eagerness to accept the challenge overlooked the obvious fact – an interview needs to be the place where they love you and do their best to be polite and smooch you into the business. If they're arguing on a good day, what would they be like on a bad day?

The answer was *very bad*. Every move I made, they unwound. Every step I took was criticised and changed. Every attempt to treat people with respect and dignity was met with board level incredulity – the staff were seen as people who removed profit from the director's pockets, rather than enabled its acquisition.

The day of my dismissal ended on a genuinely friendly note when my supervisor saw me packing up the contents of my desk and said:

'Oh, sorry that you're going. At least they liked you! They get rid of managers before Christmas if they don't like them and get rid of them in January if they do like them.'

It was January, so my luck was in! They liked me enough to sack me after I had spent out on Christmas. How thoughtful!

I tell the story because I now count myself to be fortunate to have lost my job on a regular basis, because it taught me self-reliance and helped to lay the foundations for a happy and successful career. We're allowed to make mistakes in life and, given that we don't really get to practice having a day job until we actually have a job, it is genuinely hard to know what our working styles are until we're in situ and maturing quickly. In the first 8 years of my career I learnt that:

A. **I'm the common denominator** – several businesses were as happy to wave goodbye to me as they were to hire me. I could grumble about it, or I could choose to accept the fact and find out where I was going wrong. Eventually I accepted that they did keep choosing *me* to go!

B. **I'm a good person with skill and talent** – this was confirmed when on at least two occasions the boss who had picked me for redundancy in a completely fair and in no way biased process found themselves in hot water shortly afterwards. One ex-company found out belatedly that 'that nuisance Richard, who has ideas, tries to change things and is abrasive sometimes' turned out also to be 'that hard worker Richard who kept the factory planned and organised'.

C. **It can take a few false starts to find out about yourself and what you like and what you're good at.** As part of being a management trainee I had a go at production planning, which entailed reading long lists of numbers and deciding whether the computer system was telling the truth, or having to physically count the stock to unmask its blatant lies. Seeing that I could handle a few numbers I was asked to become a trainee accountant, which I gladly accepted, having noticed that the Finance Manager had a shiny red BMW. Clearly if I worked hard I could have one of those too! The reality was somewhat less glamorous – I now had even more numbers to play with and my need for creative work was stifled. I also found out that I was hampered by mild dyscalculia (a bit like numerical dyslexia) and I would copy out the number 798,435 and write it into my spreadsheet as 789,453 and of course not notice. The extremely patient Finance Manager would be exasperated when the sheets didn't add up properly and I couldn't find the mistakes. Failing my accountancy exam was a life saver, as I was freed from the finance department and then from my job, thanks to my first taste of redundancy.

D. **You have to listen to people.** The person in question might be your partner gently telling you that they knew this role wasn't really for you all along, or it could be a line manager explaining why you didn't get the promotion you thought was certain to be yours. Feedback is information and we do need to collect it and consider it, however hurt our pride might be. I've been told by a HR Director that I wasn't bright enough to be a consultant and by a Senior Consultant that I wasn't mature enough to be a consultant. I was also told that I was good enough to be a Managing Director, but that I had none of the skill or tact or experience needed to get me there. I can't pretend that this feedback was all welcomed at the time, but I did digest it and realised that I needed to make my own luck and also needed formal training to plug the gaps and smooth off the decidedly jagged edges.

E. **It is possible to change course.** I started in factories sweeping floors and shifting boxes, and ended up as the General Manager of a factory before my 30th birthday. I had my dream job, but eventually realised that it wasn't really what I wanted to do. Having decided that I had had enough of working for other people, I set up a company to pursue my love of business coaching and management training. These course changes have been helped by further study and by coming to terms with the fact that I was not cut out for corporate life on a five-day-a-week basis. I was a good GM, but I'm a *great* coach. I can bring my creativity and intense thinking skills into focus during a session and then can leave before I start to get bored, and before people get bored of me.[3]

F. **Loving what you do matters.** In the section above I said that I love being a business coach. This isn't an idle boast; it's the best job I've ever had and after 11 years I get as much of a thrill working with a new client as I did on my first day. The point of loving something is that although you work just as hard, it feels like you're in the right place. This is why I always thought I'd had a rubbish career – I was in the wrong job and couldn't excel at it. As a coach I have excelled and produced great results, and as an aside, I've learnt that it's okay to be proud of that and to champion the successful application of my skills. You can be proud of yourself too! It makes such a difference. What are you brilliant at?

[3] Business coaching covers a wide area. I tend to work mostly as an executive development specialist and combine Lean thinking with Transactional Analysis and my own models. Please feel free to check out the information at www.richardmaun.com – you're welcome to contact me and share your story too!

G. **That it will turn out alright in the end.** It helps if you accept all of the above and persistently make your own luck by saying 'yes' when you're scared and really mean 'no'. I used to start each year by thinking 'Phew, I'm glad last year and all of its challenges are behind me – at least I can cruise a bit this year.' How naïve was I!? Each new year presented me with fresh challenges until I realised that that is how life is. There is no plateau. Sometimes I wish I could go back to younger Rich in his 20s, bored and wondering if he would be stuck in a tedious job for 40 years, enjoying the company of his colleagues, but wasting away and too frightened to quit. I'd put my arm round his shoulder, give him a loving squeeze and tell him that luckily his *inability* to shine brightly there will mean that he eventually ends up in a job he's great at and all will be well. I'd also tell him that without all the ups and downs, misfires, development courses, stressful days, lessons learnt and decisions made he would never have enjoyed the great career that he has had so far – he really would have had a rubbish career.

WE ALL HAVE MAGIC

My list of jobs over 25 years reads: floor sweeper, quality assistant, trainee manager, production planner, business development manager, general manager, business coach, visiting lecturer, programme director, executive development specialist, conference speaker, business author, radio host. These last four I combine into a portfolio career, which means that I now have the breadth and depth of creativity and variety that was lacking on day one. I couldn't have done any of these jobs on day one as I really was far too immature and lacking in awareness. I realise now of course, that all this while I have been *riding the rocket* and managing my own modern career. Also, I am struck that my current coaching role hadn't been invented in its modern form 30 years ago – so how could I have discussed that sort of career path at school anyway?

I share my story here because it's the story of a person who kept going. We all have skill and talent and can be resourceful and get the support we need to make the changes we want. In reading my story you can think about what you have learnt for yourself so far and think about how far you have come, or give yourself permission to be resourceful and begin a new chapter in your modern career.

EXERCISE – YOUR JOURNEY SO FAR

Having read about me and my 'rubbish career', take some time to think about your own career to date. Sit back in your chair and remind yourself when you smiled as you read my story and agreed with it, or what memories and thoughts it triggered for you. Make some notes in the box on the following page and celebrate being reflective, because a modern career without reflection is just a headlong dash into the side of mountain – it feels great right up to the moment you smash into the rock and the world goes very still and silent.

YOUR LIFE – YOUR CAREER REFLECTION
1. List out the job titles you've had so far:
2. What's your favourite job so far?
3. What's missing from the list?
4. Where would you like to be in *two* jobs' time?
5. What would you say to your younger self?

SO WHAT?

The message contained within this chapter is that we are all good people who don't start from a perfect place of knowledge and ability – we get thrown into work after the end of formal education, or we start because our life circumstances dictate that we must work to eat. It's okay for us to celebrate where we are, rather than cursing and wishing we were in a different place today. The past is behind us and the only things we can do are to make the most of the moment, plan for the future and start to make new decisions.

It doesn't matter where you are in your career and what you originally planned to do – we can all make changes and find a place that works for us. Of course, there are some choices which are easier to make than others. It's easier for me, for example, to move back into line management than it would be for me to retrain as a brain surgeon. However, we can limit ourselves and focus on the negatives rather than the positives. As we've already seen, I used to say that I had a rubbish career, instead of reminding myself that I had worked hard for many years, had coped successfully with redundancy, had made my own luck and had kept adjusting the flight of my rocket until it was flying in a direction that was more satisfying to me.

This leads us to the key question in this chapter:

HOW DO YOU TEND TO FRAME YOUR CAREER?

If we change the way we frame things, we change how we feel about them, which will tend to lead new thoughts, new decisions and new actions. I tend to think now that my career wasn't rubbish at all – it just took me a few years of experimenting and confidence building to realise that I needed to make big changes or I would go nowhere. As a result I'm now not so hard on myself as I used to be. We are all allowed to learn and to take time to make sense of where we are and what needs to change. In my case, I went back to university and studied for a post-graduate qualification and that propelled me out of the middle of the office, away from my hometown and into a bright new world of fun. But that's another story!

LEARNING EXERCISE

Career Framing
Think about the question on the previous page and then circle the answers that apply to you:

(A) How do I describe my career, so far, to myself?	(B) How do I describe my career so far to friends and confidants?
Successful – I'm on track and having fun.	**Successful** – I'm on track and having fun.
Good enough – I'm doing well and still need to fine tune it a bit.	**Good enough** – I'm doing well and still need to fine tune it a bit.
Right job wrong place – I need to look for somewhere else.	**Right job wrong place** – I need to look for somewhere else.
Stalled – I find it difficult to motivate myself and need to take stock of my career.	**Stalled** – I find it difficult to motivate myself and need to take stock of my career.
Rubbish – I am in the wrong job and need to own up to how unhappy I really am and make some changes.	**Rubbish** – I am in the wrong job and need to own up to how unhappy I really am and make some changes.

If there is a difference between the answers in both columns, what deeper truth am I tending to overlook? (For example, am I a frustrated musician wanting to hit the road, or do I want to go back to school and study for a different qualification?)

What is one simple step I can take to improve my career?

4
Modern Career Thinking
– Key Skills For Success –

COCKPIT QUESTION:
What will you do to take responsibility for your modern career?

WE ARE ALL RIDING *OUR OWN* ROCKET

Like it or not, we are all career pilots. Each of us is riding our career rocket towards retirement and we need to understand the nature of careers and have the essential flight control skills to keep us safe and in control.

AN ESSENTIAL PERMISSION

This is a truth:

The responsibility for our modern career is ours and ours alone. Therefore, we have permission to manage our lives for our benefit.

It's our life. We have control!

UNIT OF ONE

Each of us is a unit of one at work. This means we are an economic unit of production, the smallest machine in the organisation. It doesn't matter whether we work for a not-for-profit organisation; we attract costs and we have an impact on the well-being, customer service and output that our organisation seeks to have. We might be part of a team and work effectively within that, but we are still a unit of one, like a cog in a gear chain – we can be replaced for a better performing component if the organisation wants to realise new benefits. We are not indispensable and it doesn't matter how senior we are, we can all be replaced.

The rise in ideas such as 'bring your own device to work' is good evidence that we are a unit of one. Organizations that utilise this idea ask employees to source their own computers and bring them in, instead of issuing them with corporate items chosen centrally.

Being a unit of one also means that we have to focus on ourselves – it's up to us to get the training we need, generate opportunities for ourselves and make sure that our working life is as we want it to be. Plenty of people (myself included) have remained in an organisation because of the people there and then when forced to move, have found more fulfilling work and equally friendly people. Crucially in these cases, people do not ask to go back to the old place – they instinctively know that voluntarily moving back to a less fulfilling job is the rocket-riding equivalent of switching the engine off and hoping something good will happen. It won't.

IT'S OKAY TO BE SELF-INTERESTED

We don't have to be selfish or mean-spirited to be successful as a unit of one – the world is always a happier place to live when we have a tolerant and pleasant disposition. To mistake a self-interested approach for a selfish approach would be to misunderstand the subtlety of life. Self-interested means that we take note of our needs and set out to meet them. We might be competitive, we might be first in the queue and we might nudge others to make sure things happen for us in the way we want them to. This is perfectly reasonable. Selfish, on the other hand, implies that we take care of ourselves regardless of others.

Being self-interested says that we can take notice of others *and* be polite *and* we don't have to wait for them – they can be self-interested in their life too. We don't have to manage their lives for them, that's *their* job. Ours is to manage our own and not to fall into the trap of being first in the queue, only to hold the door open for everyone behind us and then find out that there are no seats left for us.

PRIDE IS POWER

We can be powerful in our life by being proud of who we are and what we have achieved. We may have inherited intelligence, good looks, long limbs and great health. Those are given. It's what we do with our inheritance that counts and if we're not proud of ourselves, then what's the point of doing anything if we don't take some pleasure in it? We may as well not bother. When working with executives, I often ask them what they are proud of and the most predictable answer they give me includes the majority of the following nonsense:

'I'm very proud of what my team has achieved. They've worked so hard and produced a strong performance this year, meeting key performance targets and delivering bottom line profits, while maintaining our stakeholder values and increasing our customer satisfaction index.'

What?!

Is that how you measure your worth and time spent? Only by your team's output? If you did nothing then your organisation may as well keep your salary next year and make further savings. There's also the depressing reality that, for some people, jargon is the way they measure their lives and successes. They work 80 hours a week to 'improve a customer satisfaction index'. What rubbish! They need to remember that they're human and instead of talking management twaddle, ought to smile and reply:

'Well Richard, through my structured and supportive leadership, including effective goal setting, I have made my team happy and I have made more of our customers happy. This means that when they go home at night they have a happier family life, are nicer to their kids and smile more, have less stress and may live longer. And I am proud of that.'

Now *that* is something to be proud of and worth working hard to achieve. We mustn't lose sight of *ourselves* in the rush to find a job, get a job, keep a job, get promoted and keep delivering value.

THE BIRTH OF THE MODERN CAREER

Forget the idea of a career ladder and the notion that we are somehow open to having a traditional career. That concept bit the dust when typewriters were replaced by computers and secretaries replaced with... nothing. Overnight, we all became able to write our own letters and later, with the rise of email, we didn't need to walk round the organisation, our words became mobile and our feet became static. Interestingly, the first email in the UK was sent by the Queen on 26th March 1976 and it said 'Popping out with the corgis to get a paper. Back later Phil. Lol. ERII ☺'.[4]

Better, faster and more accurate communication has perhaps been the most useful factor in developing the working world over the last 30 years. People are now much freer to work where they like, are more accountable for the work they do and can share ideas and collaborate more quickly. Generations Y and Z (who we will meet later) talk less about teamwork (a tired 80's concept) and more about collaboration (a fresh, modern approach that celebrates thinking and the pooling of talent). Teamwork used to be a synonym for 'doing what the boss wanted, keeping quiet and waiting for the slowest person to catch up'. Who wants teamwork when we can have collaboration?

GLOBAL TRENDS

Global trends and cultural shifts matter. In today's world, these are the new words that are shaping our culture and our economies:

[4]   The date and person are certainly correct. The message may not be...

TRENDS THAT MATTER
- Globalisation
- Collaboration
- Social Media
- Flexibility
- Renewable Energy
- Personal Responsibility

These are the ideas that are shaping our careers, as economies and governments respond to social and industrial developments. If we want to remain successful in our modern career, we need to be aware of the possibilities and opportunities that these ideas will create.

Consider social media. When pitching for a book contract one question you are likely to be asked now is 'How large is your platform?' The publisher is keen to know how many people you are connected to, because that sets up an expectation for how many books you personally might sell through your own network. We have to remember that the goal of social media interaction isn't the acquisition of huge volumes of contacts per se – we need to talk to people and engage with them. It's better to have 100 people with whom you engage and have good rapport with, than an impressive sounding 100,000 contacts that actually only contains 20 friends and 99,980 spambots, broadcast engines and remote celebrities.

In our modern career we need to embrace the key trends and new ideas because we need to keep building for the future. If we don't then we could be left high and dry when we need to find a new source of income.

You might be wondering what 'renewable energy' has to do with careers. This is on the list because it's driving a whole group of technological developments (although some would argue they may not be improvements) that are having profound effects on the world economy. The rise in new methods of harnessing renewable energy sources, such as wind, wave and sunlight, has also spurred petrochemical industries to find new ways of exploiting non-renewable resources (which until the price of oil went up, were previously not commercially viable to exploit). In 1970, the price of a barrel of crude oil was $15 and in 2011, that same barrel was worth $90. One result of this has been to shift manufacturing output back to the USA from China.[5]

Energy costs have reduced in the USA thanks to the exploitation of shale gas reserves, which are helpfully located in sparsely populated areas, making hydraulic fracturing a more viable option. This means that instead of using China as a manufacturing base and investing energy and cost into shipping, it's becoming more economical to build items in the States and take advantage of lower local energy costs and avoid the time and complexity of long distance out-sourced production. Cars and computers are in the vanguard of this trend and both Apple and General Motors are beginning to bring manufacturing home from overseas.

---

[5]   Reference: www.wtrg.com – Oil price history and analysis.

TAKE ME HOME TABLE[6]

The modern career is here to stay – we are effectively in Career 2.0 territory, where the traditional career has been replaced by the vastly improved, rebooted, personally configured modern career version. In order to illustrate what that means in practical terms, here is a *Take Me Home Table* for you to consider, that shows us what we need to know and demonstrate in order to be successful.

For your reference, the *7 Tenets of Modern Careers* were first featured in the book **Bouncing Back**, as were the *Internal/External/Specialist Skills*. The *Organisational Impact Score* forms one of the central themes to the book **How to Keep Your Job**, which details what you need to do to work effectively. You are welcome to explore these books, add them to your career management library and increase your store of practical tools and concepts.

---

[6]   A 'Take Me Home Table' is my term for a useful item that needs to be cut out and kept, referred to at least once a week and moved from the book into our conscious mind. It's one of those useful nuggets that we want close by and ready to help us.

TAKE ME HOME TABLE – THE ESSENTIAL GUIDE TO A SUCCESSFUL MODERN CAREER

7 TENETS OF A MODERN CAREER			
1. Knowing our own competencies	2. Having great job hunting skills	3. Being able to retrain	4. Being able to work in a variety of ways
5. Being responsible for our money management	6. Not knowing where our career will be when we retire		7. Not knowing when retirement will be
MODERN CAREER SKILLS			
External Skills 1. Productivity 2. People Skills 3. Public Relations These multiply to give us our *Organisational Impact Score*, which is a useful measure of added value.	**Internal Skills** 1. Agility 2. Determination 3. Humility 4. Learning 5. Reliability 6. Resilience 7. Thinking	**Specialist Skills** 1. Technical language 2. Trade skills 3. Process skills	
6 CAREER CHALLENGES			
1. To do the job we're paid for	2. To keep developing	3. To maintain our energy	
4. To remain open minded	5. To think forwards	6. To be true to ourselves	

The table shows the top level items that we need to pay attention to. The other chapters in *Riding the Rocket* consider other aspects of our working life, such as the impact of technology and the money vs. happiness question in more detail. If we have the top level in sight then we will tend to be more resourceful and will ask better questions of ourselves and others.

7 TENETS OF A MODERN CAREER

1. **Knowing our own competencies** – we need to know what we are naturally good at and where we excel, because if we play to those strengths, we will tend to perform to a higher standard, even when we feel tired or are under pressure.

2. **Having great job hunting skills** – we will change jobs perhaps 10 or more times in our working lives and will need the skills to network and be successful at competency-based interviews. If we learn to drive, to cook, to be a great mum or dad, why is it that so many people still trust to luck when it comes to job hunting skills? If you want to reduce your stress and be more confident throughout life, acquire relevant skills and you'll be surprised how much of a difference it makes.

3. **Being able to retrain** – modern careers allow us to move away from our original profession and try something new. It doesn't matter what we start out as; people often fall into a job because it follows on from school, or they had a friend who sorted them out. What counts is that *if* we want to change, we can.

4. **Being able to work in a variety of ways** – this means that we can be a regular employee, set up our own business, form a

partnership, or have a combination that works for us in the form of a portfolio lifestyle.

5. **Being responsible for our money management** – we need to do more than make plans for our retirement (be it equity release or savings plan, as pensions are struggling to remain viable in the face of long-term low interest rates). We need to budget for training and development, for example. This also means having a cash buffer in place to take the sting out of redundancy and enable us to spend at least 6 months looking for our next role.

6. **Not knowing where our career will be when we retire** – the future can't be predicted and we only have to consider the recent rise of tablet computers to see the truth in that. Apple's revolutionary iPad was much derided as a giant smartphone or a tiny laptop – that is, until people used it and realised it was perfect for media consumption. In career terms, we don't know when we'll get a breakthrough, or have the success that makes our name – all we can do is to keep going and enjoy the ride.

7. **Not knowing when retirement will be** – the idea of being forced to retire at a specific age is now rapidly being consigned to history, as people have better long-term health care and are able to live more productive lives for a longer period of time. This of course also relates to the decline in pensions and the need for us all to keep working for as long as we need to financially.

3 KEY SKILL GROUPS

A. **External Skills** – these are the ones that keep us in a role or, if we lack them, cause us to get fired. Our *Organisational Impact*

Score is the amount of productivity we deliver, multiplied by the amount of people skills we exhibit, multiplied by the public relations we create for ourselves.

1. **Productivity** – our ability to complete tasks on time and to the required standard. We also need to be consistent or we become a 'zero sum person' when the bad days cancel out the good ones. This could lead to problems because a zero sum person is a waste of money and the organisation may as well save our salary.

2. **People Skills** – our ability to be consistently friendly, approachable and considerate of others. Do we argue for the fun of it? Pick fault and magnify tiny errors? Do we smile and say 'hello' to people and radiate warmth? Are we approachable and pleasant to work with when trying to solve a problem? Again, we need to be consistent, because smiling one day and then being a grumpy grouch for the rest of the week isn't going to make us many friends. Would you like to work with you, given the choice?

3. **Public Relations** – an area that is often overlooked. What do people say about us behind our back? Do we share good news with our line manager and make it clear what our part was in the success? What friends and allies do we have in high places? Given that we are a unit of one it's okay to make sure people see the best of us and are reminded about our contribution to the success of the organisation. If they don't know what we add then it's easier for them to get rid of us.

To find your *Organisational Impact Score*, have a go at completing the following sum:

ORGANISATIONAL IMPACT SCORE

Use the sum to find your score

Productivity self-score out of 20
x
People skills self-score out of 15
x
Public relations self-score out of 10

= ?/20 x ?/15 x ?/10

= _____

Your total score divided by 3,000

For example, your scores might be as follows: 10 x 8 x 5 = 400 ÷ 3,000 = 0.133.

People doing this sum quickly realise that what is important is not to be great in just one area, but to be great in *all* areas, because one low score can negatively affect the overall score.

Our score then places us in one of three zones. Where are you?

1. **Keeper Zone.** If we score between 1.000 and 0.420 then we're in the high performing *Keeper Zone* and are doing a great job. There is no guarantee that we'll be employed forever, but there will probably be other less value-adding staff who may be fired first. Being here means that we tend to be consistent,

pleasant and assertive – and are more likely to be promoted and offered interesting new projects to work on.

2. **Cruiser Zone.** If we score between 0.420 and 0.040 then we're in the *Cruiser Zone*, where the majority of people spend most of their working lives. We're not super-high flyers and we're not causing a problem. However, our score relative to our colleagues does matter because people with lower scores are more likely to be fired from the organisation. We need to be vigilant and ensure our scores stay as high as possible and not sleepwalk our way into a problem.

3. **Cutter Zone.** If we score between 0.040 and 0.000 then we are in the *Cutter Zone*, which means we have one foot outside the door, or need to seek immediate support. Our overall performance will need to dramatically improve if we want to stay. Improvements are possible and sometimes all it takes is a new role, change of working hours, or a fresh start under a new manager for us to excel again. If we're in this zone we need to face up to the reality of our situation, make a significant change in our working environment, or begin to prepare for our next job hunt.

Now that we know our score and the zone we sit in, we need to reflect on our performance and decide to change one thing for the better. Perhaps we need to increase our public relations score and celebrate success more often?

B. **Internal Skills**

These are the skills that relate to how we think, how we feel and how we view our place in the world.

1. **Agility** – how well do we respond to change? Do we grumble, or do we seek to understand change and look for a positive outcome for us?

2. **Determination** – this is our will to succeed. Are we tough operators who like to finish a task or do we give up when we go over a little bump in the road and wail that life is too hard?

3. **Humility** – an essential ingredient of success. This doesn't mean being a pushover. It means knowing our limits and apologising if we cross them. It also means asking good questions and seeking to engage other people's thinking rather than assume we have all the answers ourselves.

4. **Learning** – how good we are at taking on new skills. A 'learning mindset' is a prized asset because employers can work with us in the future and aren't constrained by the level of skill we bring to the organisation on day one.

5. **Reliability** – can we be trusted to complete work? Is our desk such a mess that any piece of new paper on it is immediately lost in the jungle, or are we organised, punctual and present?

6. **Resilience** – this is the ability to soak up problems and find solutions. It's also how we cope with setbacks and false starts – do we complain or do we learn from the experience and devise a new plan?

7. **Thinking** – my favourite skill because it underpins so much else. How much time do we take to think? Or do we think

that thinking is a waste of time and *action* is much better? When we do think, it's worth listing at least three options to avoid a snap decision and to make sure we have key facts to support our decision. Plenty of people *think* they're thinking, when in fact they're simply rubber stamping decisions which their subconscious made a while ago.

C. Specialist Skills

Specialist skills are the ones we need, in order to do the job to a high standard. We may need to undergo specialist training, attend revision courses, or maintain continuous personal development (CPD) plans. If we know our business or industry at a detailed level and can talk confidently about trends and new developments, then our interest will percolate into good PR for us. Specialist skills include:

1. **Technical language** – the words we need to communicate effectively.
2. **Trade skills** – specific abilities we need to do our job effectively.
3. **Process skills** – general support skills, such as presenting, selling or using a computer.

6 CAREER CHALLENGES

1. **To do the job we're paid for** – it may sound almost too simple to be worth mentioning, but if we wander off course then the organisation will quickly tire of us.
2. **To keep developing** – there is never an 'end point', unless we have retired and hung up our tool bag.

3. **To maintain our energy** – we must take good care of our health and make sure we have the energy to keep working and delivering value. There are many people who have seen their parents retire at 65 and who don't know what it is like to keep working until they're 70. That's five years of extra 'work health' that we need, in order to keep feeding ourselves. The current generations are going to find out what that's like for themselves.

4. **To remain open-minded** – we don't have to like new inventions but we can at least seek to understand them. We may be sad if our career falters, and that's understandable, but we can continue to look at new options and take positive steps towards a brighter future.

5. **To think forwards** – too many people think backwards and spend their time comparing what happened in the 'good old days' to their current situation. This is a waste of energy and our time is better spent thinking about where we might be in two years' time and considering useful career questions, such as: What plans to do we need to develop to get there? Who can support us on the journey? What are the key 'play or pass' decisions that we will face?

4. **To be true to ourselves** – this is a sentiment that crops up throughout the other chapters. This is a book to support you in your career and me in mine (I use everything I write about) and as we are two different people we will have our own likes and desires and ambitions. A colleague of mine left a great job in a factory that I managed, to set up her floristry business. When she handed in her resignation I was shocked – she was

a talented worker and on track to be a manager fairly quickly. She thanked me for trying to persuade her to stay, but was adamant that she was leaving. 'I need to go,' she said with feeling, 'it's where my heart lies.' You can't argue with that.

CASE STUDY – JUSTIN: GREAT PR

Justin is a senior manager for a large printing contractor who is responsible for managing a team of over 50 operators, including printers and technicians. He started as a printer and then moved into management and he commands the respect of his team because he listens to them and is interested in his industry on a general level. An example of career-enhancing public relations occurred when I met with the director he reports to, who went out of his way to tell me about Justin's performance at a recent meeting.

The meeting had been convened to discuss long-range planning issues and consider how staffing levels could be affected, what action the organisation needed to take, or at least put on file for the future. One of Justin's colleagues had prepared a report, but couldn't answer detailed questions and had clearly done the bare minimum of work required for the task.

When this colleague faltered under questioning from the director, Justin smoothly stepped in and lucidly talked through the prevailing political climate, developing trends and what they could do to address critical issues. It was a masterful performance and delivered with genuine interest, that showed how much he enjoyed working in that industry and how widely he read. However, that wasn't the point of re-telling this story. It was the director's comment that really showed the enormous public relations victory that Justin had scored that day, when he commented with a broad smile:

'I had *no idea* Justin was so well read and took such an interest. His knowledge was *amazing!*'

When was the last time you amazed your line manager?

CASE STUDY –
MELANIE: PEOPLE SKILLS IMPACTING PR

Sometimes we don't realise that the way we work has a cumulative effect on people. For example, if we argue with a colleague on Monday and apologise on Tuesday it's likely that the argument is still logged deep in our subconscious. It might be tagged as 'resolved', but that doesn't mean it has been disposed of – a tiny piece of 'argument-energy' often remains in the memory, like a tiny splatter of ink on a white piece of paper. Sometimes, if the apology is particularly effective – a bunch of pretty flowers, a cream cake the size of a bus, or us making tea for a week – the argument may be fully rendered harmless and all is well.

Melanie was a senior clerk in an insurance company and worked well with her team leader, who said that she was keen to promote her to the next level, but never managed to get round to doing so. After the third one-to-one where this issue had arisen, Melanie's frustration got the better of her and she blurted out, 'Why won't you promote me, Louise? You keep saying I'm good enough. What's the problem?'

'The problem, Melanie, is that I don't trust you,' Louise replied sincerely and without malice. 'I need to know that you will support me when I'm not around and uphold decisions, and not join in with the banter from the team. When you're being cynical, it looks like you're really disagreeing with me and if we're going to work together more closely I need to know that you're reliable and will support me. You might not like a particular policy decision, but you do have to promote it to the team.'

Melanie thought about it and realised that her 'cynical humour', as she liked to call it, had gradually undermined the relationship she had with her boss. She hadn't meant that to happen, but the cumulative effect had been to sow seeds of doubt. She owned up to her behaviour (humility in action), thanked Louise for the feedback and promised to change her ways. Two weeks later she was called into the office by Louise and promoted, having been able to demonstrate her loyalty in two team meetings.

The word 'loyalty' isn't meant to sound sinister here, rather it reflects the fact that people require clear support. If management decisions have been made in good faith it can be destabilising and disruptive if line leaders and supervisors join in with the grumbles of the staff. Melanie's story also illustrates two other important points about managing our modern career:

- Productivity, people skills and public relations are connected and affect one another, for good or for bad.
- When we are handed a decisive *play or pass moment* our career-rocket momentarily hangs suspended in mid-air, waiting for the outcome of the conversation or decision. Do we play or pass? What happens next is up to us, but these are the moments that last mere seconds but will define the path of our lives.

SO WHAT?

Modern careers are here to stay and it's up to us whether we choose to ignore them or to embrace them, and to keep track of how well we apply the skills, tools and thinking in this chapter. In three months' time, after we have read this book and put it back on the shelf, we need to remember what has shifted in our thinking about careers and the nature of managing our *own* career.

Choose wisely. I learnt the hard way that if I was deaf and blind to my own failings I would lose my job. They did *choose* me to leave, it was never an accident. When I finally woke up to this my attitude changed – I switched on to the reality of a modern career and have enjoyed a successful period of riding the rocket ever since.

LEARNING EXERCISE

1. Take a step toward riding your rocket in a thoughtful and productive way. Re-read this chapter and notice what has stuck when you return to this point. It might be words, a phrase or a combination of things. You can let your intuition guide you.
2. Once you have noticed what is resonating within you please open your diary, be it electronic or paper, and note it down on two dates – three months and six months later.
3. This will give you two reminders that will pop up when you have forgotten about them and two chances for you to revisit the learning and cement it in to your conscious memory.
4. Then give yourself a small treat for being proactive.

5
Awareness Please
– Don't Be A Tourist –

COCKPIT QUESTION:
How will you take better care of yourself?

REALITY CHECK

Are you comfortable? Is the room at the right temperature or are you a little cold? Could you do with a drink, or do you need to put the book down and make a snack? Maybe a delicious cheese sandwich would do. Fresh crusty bread, crisp green lettuce and generous slices of gently matured cheddar cheese would be good right now. Cut the sandwich in half and notice the colour and the smell. If you want to you can put the book down now, run into the kitchen and make yourself a sneaky snack. If you don't, then then the chances are that as you read the rest of this chapter, you'll be distracted by the imagined smell and taste of bread and cheese.

Awareness changes things. Without it we bumble through

life and with it we can move mountains and make our life what we want it to be.

TOURISM IS FOR TOURISTS

If you're on holiday and want to take in as much of the world as you can in ten action-packed days then be my guest. Be a tourist and go wild. Pack a camera and take at least three photographs of each location to show the grandchildren in later years how much of the world you have seen.

When it comes to our career though, we need to be more thoughtful and less rushed. If we intend to plough through our life at top speed, then it won't be much of a life, in the same way that rushing a rich meal just gives us indigestion and a nagging sense that, yet again, we did this to ourselves.

Fly too fast and we might miss opportunities or make hasty decisions. Fly too slow and we'll fall out of the sky, so dawdling isn't an option either. We need to fly at a speed that is safe and at which we can handle the controls. Being a tourist is for holiday time – the rest of the time we need to go through life at a fair pace, yet stop sometimes and enjoy what we have or simply take an extra break now again and look around us.

THE ENEMIES OF AWARENESS

We are all good people and whatever job we do, whatever our domestic situation and wherever we live, we all have clouds around us that block the visibility out of the windows of our rocket. We can relax and remind ourselves that we are perfectly normal people going about our business in the only way we know how. We've never been this age before, so how do we know how to behave? We don't! We can only notice where we are, what is around us and be thoughtful about what we can do about it. Part of this process is about being aware of what the *enemies of awareness* are – which sounds like a great piece of circular thinking! How can we break this circle and keep ourselves in good shape? The answer is to look at the clouds in more detail and see what is creating them.

> **THE ENEMIES OF AWARENESS INCLUDE:**
> - Fatigue
> - Fear
> - Stress
> - Inexperience
> - Lack of Interest
> - Filtering

Please note; the word 'fear' is used here to denote a scale from mild anxiety all the way to being deeply scared. We filter things when we're afraid, or to prevent the feeling from increasing. However, we also filter a wide range of stimuli. In this section, therefore, fear is the *emotion* we feel, and filtering is the *process* of sieving out items of information.

ENEMY NO.1 – FATIGUE

How long is your day? Maybe 18 hours or 20 hours from sleep-to-sleep? With the rise of smartphones and tablets, people are now able to take work to bed with them in a way they'd have laughed at a few years ago. Emails, texts and tweets roll in round the clock and clog up the inbox of our lives.

For the majority of our time, we live in a sleep-deprived state and take performance enhancing 'drugs' to get us through the day. The rise of designer coffee shops and the invention of the double espresso skinny latte mocha choca mind blaster is testament to the fact that we are trading sleep for drugs and working ever harder to find the money to pay for our daily booster on the way to work.

When we are fatigued our responses slow down and our thinking dulls. We wouldn't dare drink and drive, but many people will regularly drive in a state of extreme tiredness and will underestimate the effects of fatigue on their road sense and reaction speed.

ANTIDOTES TO FATIGUE

1. **Rhythms.** We need to make sure we understand our natural rhythms so that we work when we're productive and rest when we're not. Are you a morning lark or a night owl? Does your job push you in the opposite direction to your natural inclination? If you can, change your hours or schedule work so that you can take advantage of your best times when your performance will increase and you will have less fatigue.
2. **Sleep.** More sleep = clearer thinking, more resilience and less raw emotion.
3. **Hobbies.** I was asked once what my hobbies were and realised that I didn't have any when the interviewer said, 'No, Richard, writing is work, what else do you do?' That made me think and now I have a bass guitar to play and a radio show to have fun with. How do you spend your free time? What new hobby can you take up this year?

ENEMY NO.2 – FEAR

We all get scared; it's a basic human emotion. Extreme fear can incapacitate us and even though externally we may be looking thoughtful and cheerful, inside we are frozen like a statue and unable to make our legs work, or recall the brilliant opening to our speech.

When thinking about riding the rocket, it's hard to keep our eyes open and focussed on the task ahead when it involves something scary like coping with redundancy, going for a job interview, or presenting our case for promotion to the senior managers. The fear overwhelms us and we avoid the task, claim we're sick, or simply resign ourselves to a career that we don't really want. It's okay to be scared. We have plenty of examples in our lives when the moment *after* the scare was something utterly magical that we wouldn't change for the world, such as proposing to our girlfriend or watching our first baby being delivered. There are times when we're scared and get through it nonetheless. It's the same for our modern career – the fear is there to make us stop and think, to get help, to practice and to take care of ourselves.

ANTIDOTES TO FEAR

1. **Facts.** We often scare ourselves with thinking that turns the seed of a problem into a towering beanstalk of a nightmare. We use our 'logic' to extrapolate a line of reasoning and reach a conclusion that sounds plausible and frightening to us. But we can understand that 'internal logic' isn't objective and ruthlessly clinical; it's often a mixture of prejudices and assumptions. To counter this, we need to write down the facts and then generate three different scenarios. Once we have these, we can easily see which ones tend towards high or low risk and where our preferences lie.

2. **Talk.** We tend to keep things to ourselves; worrying that sharing them will make us appear weak or needy to others. These are pejorative words that mask our real needs and have no basis in reality. We're good people who can be resourceful and get help when we need it. Often the best kind of support is to talk with an impartial coach or mentor, who can listen and offer us rational observations and new courses of action to allay our fears and make it safe for us.

3. **Bridge.** When describing a situation to others, we often use scary words that magnify the risk. For example, we might say 'I need to jump the gap' or 'I need to let go and see what happens'. Both of these sentences make the situation sound just about as scary as possible – we are hard-wired not to jump or let go, which is why we tend to steer away from cliffs and use the stairs, rather than leaping off a roof. Instead, we can build a bridge in our language and say, 'I'm going to take small simple steps' or 'I'm going to keep one foot on solid ground and test the water with one toe at a time'. By changing our words we automatically replace our fear with a sense of *possibility*.

ENEMY NO.3 – STRESS

A training supervisor once asked me when I felt stressed in my working life. My answer was that I couldn't recall specific moments, but would perhaps feel a bit stressed when driving to see a new client. The supervisor smiled and surprised me by suggesting that we all tend to operate under stress from the moment we wake up to the moment we go to sleep. This is because we have to cope with time pressures that constrain us – rushing to shower and get breakfast, getting the children ready, grabbing our briefcase, heading out of the door to complete the school run and then charging into our place of work. And that's just our first waking hour. If we think of ourselves as a plank supported by a stool at either end, stress is the weight that pushes down in the middle, causing the plank to bend and creak and maybe snap.

When we're stressed, our clear thinking is curtailed. We become irritable and restless as we struggle to reconcile the knot in our head with the load pushing down on our shoulders and the need to keep going in the moment. From a career perspective, the irony is that many people will set themselves up to be stressed by making sure they have a demanding job with a high salary and a commensurate risk of failure. I've met senior executives who wear their stress as a badge of honour – it marks them as someone to be taken seriously and enables them to steamroller people into agreements as they charge through their career.

When we're stressed, we can attract a good deal of care and attention from others who worry about us. Instead of using this as a prompt to change our lives, we get used to the attention and maintain the stress to keep getting the attention, because without it we fear that we are nothing. When executives who get fired say to me 'I lost my job, my life is over', I tend to reply with exaggerated incredulity, 'Really? Your *life* is *over*?'

There is always hope.

One of the best days of my life was when I faced up to my stress and shared my feelings about my rotten job and my rotten relationship with my rotten boss, *with* my rotten boss. He listened and agreed and the weight on my shoulders lifted. Nothing mattered any more – the invisible elephant in the room had been heavily dusted with chalk and finally made visible. Nothing could touch me and in that moment, the stress disappeared and a new career path opened up. I had ridden the rocket almost to the ground and had managed to pull up at the last minute. What a fantastic feeling that was!

ANTIDOTES TO STRESS
1. **Recognition.** We need to stop getting recognition for being stressed and instead start to get recognition for taking care of ourselves. This means eating lunch, pausing to have a drink, allowing enough travel time to arrive in a calm state and taking five minutes after lunch to read our to-do list and calmly plan our afternoon.
2. **Chalk.** Often we're stressed about a particular situation and until we 'chalk the elephant' by making specific reference to it, nothing will change. To do this effectively, it helps to plan our conversation in advance and write down the key points of what we need to say.

> 3. **Reflection**. Stress is often a by-product of our ambition, because it keeps us grinding away at a job when our health would suggest we would be better off working somewhere else. There is nothing wrong in ambition per se, as we'll see in a later chapter, but if it's blind ambition that hurts us then is that really a good thing? If we are stressed, we need to take a break, reflect for a while and think through what we're doing in this headlong rush to get somewhere.

ENEMY NO.4 – INEXPERIENCE

The goal is to maintain our awareness, so that we can effectively pilot the rocket that is our career. Yet, we have never had a career before, so how do we know what to be aware of? Hindsight is a wonderful thing once you've lived a little, but each stage of our modern career is new to us and as such we are always vulnerable to the effects of inexperience.

Three useful questions are:

- What was the biggest mistake you have made so far in your career?
- What did you learn from it?
- What advice would you give to your younger self?

In my case, my biggest mistake was assuming I could learn to be a manager on the job without any formal training or support from the business owners. Each mistake was made under the harsh glare of the senior supervisor, who eventually took pity on me and would pull me to one side to explain exactly why my new idea to improve production would not work. I learnt that my ambition lead me to take a job for which I was unsuited to at the time and since then, I've made sure that a training and support plan has been part of my first three months when embarking on a new task or job.

ANTIDOTES TO INEXPERIENCE

1. **Question.** Learning to ask great questions will unlock new opportunities for us and will fill the potholes of our mind. When I started my own business, I systematically interviewed people who were already working as executive coaches and trainers and I asked them all:
   a. What mistakes did you make in the first year of business?
   b. What technical skills do I need to do this job well?
   c. What personal/communication skills do I need to do this job well?
   d. What do you think is my most important area for development right now?
   e. What question haven't I asked you that I really need to? What questions can you ask people? How? Where? What? When? Who? (I tend to avoid asking 'why' because it can take us back to our childhood and we can get an unthinking response instead of a thoughtful one – ask 'what' instead.)
2. **Borrow.** The shortcut to overcoming inexperience is to find a role model and learn from them. If possible, observe them at work – instead of joining in you can often learn more by watching from the sides for ten minutes. Notice their body language, any key phrases that they use to get results and how they engage other people and how they manage their time.
3. **Confront.** It's tempting to let things drift by and I have been guilty of that in my early career – we hope that tomorrow will be better than today without making any changes. Instead of repetition we can confront our lack of experience, or our lack of competence, and talk to our line manager about it.

The word 'competent' may seem severe but it can apply to mundane tasks too. Being asked to prepare an important slide presentation when we have had neither the training nor any prior experience is likely to end badly for us. When we're given a task we can assert ourselves and can say 'yes I will do that *and* I would like some training first. Who is the best person to talk to?' Using *and* in this way is always assertive.

ENEMY NO.5 – LACK OF INTEREST

We've already seen that asking questions is a great way to put ourselves in awareness, but if we're not interested we're likely to be very half-hearted about it. I'm surprised by people who take only a small interest in their workplace. They walk past notice boards, rarely volunteer for extra activities and pour scorn on the monthly corporate newsletter. Interest relates to attitude, so what's your attitude to your organisation? Are you positive towards it or fed up and grumpy?

> **OUR ATTITUDE HIDES A TRUTH:**
> If we're not interested in our organisation, it won't
> be interested in us.

This is a pity because we want to have a great career! We don't want to miss out on opportunities to get involved with new projects or maybe have the chance to go on a training course or apply for a role in a different department. We need to be alive to the world around us and realise that in many cases, people fail to move their career forward because they fail to be interested in their surroundings.

As you read this do you know what's on your organisation's notice board? If you have a stack of news emails in your inbox, do you read them quickly once a week or delete them en bloc without having scanned through them?

ANTIDOTES TO LACK OF INTEREST

1. **Observe.** Take a walk round your organisation and look at the walls. Read the posters and the notices. The next time you go to a meeting, have a look at the room you're in and take an interest in what's on the walls. Your next job could be pinned up there!

2. **Befriend.** Organisations are full of people who think that they're normal – they come to work to do a good job and to earn the money to feed their families and get on in life. We can find ourselves feeling intimidated by people we don't know and of course they're just people at the end of the day! It's tempting to stick close to our current friendship group and not to talk to new people. The helpful motto here is – friendship first, sell second – we can go and talk to people and simply enjoy making friends, without worrying about needing to sell anything to them.

3. **Volunteer.** There are always opportunities to get ourselves into groups and make new connections. The best way to start is to tell your line manager that you're interested in becoming part of a process improvement group. Many organisations have these and they add value by removing wasted time and effort from overly complex procedures. Managers like them because they save time and money, so offering to *start* one is a great way to be noticed and it can introduce you to a cross-section of the organisation, bringing you to the attention of senior managers and directors.

ENEMY NO.6 – FILTERING

We filter out information and stimuli that don't fit our expected pattern of things. Sometimes this helps us to avoid an overload and sometimes it's because we want to keep out inconvenient information that would cause us to modify our plans. For example, how many times have we had a problem and ignored it in the hope that it will go away? We might also have ignored people, because acknowledging their presence means holding *that* conversation which we have been avoiding, or we go for a long walk and ignore the rain clouds that are gathering on the horizon. To see them would mean to miss our walk or would require us to retrace our steps and fetch a coat before we get soaked.

ANTIDOTES TO FILTERING

1. **Tune in.** We can take a moment to tune in to our surroundings and to notice who is there, what the weather is doing or to recap what someone has just said to us. We've already seen how observation is a powerful way to keep ourselves in awareness – when we enter a room it makes good sense to pause for a moment and notice who is there and to write down people's names and say hello to them. When someone is speaking to us we need to maintain eye contact with them and make sure we're not pretending to listen while texting our colleagues.
2. **Self-talk.** Much of our filtering is evidenced by our self-talk in that we use standard phrases that often mask the reality. A classic is saying 'I'm fine' when asked if we're hungry, stressed and so on. We tend to believe our words after a

while, and even when a close friend asks us how we are, we still say 'I'm fine'. Other clichés include 'I'm okay really' or 'it will just take five minutes' or 'I'm sure I can work it out as I go along'. We can acknowledge the truth, change our self-talk and get support instead of perpetuating the myth that we're fine, when we're not.

3. **Think.** If we take time to think, similar to when we take time to notice, then we can move ourselves into awareness. To think clearly, we can remove ourselves from our place of work for five minutes and pace up and down, letting our legs burn off nervous energy so that our brains can get a grip on the situation we're facing.

CASE STUDY – TERRY

This chapter is about awareness because to ride our rocket we need to be able to notice the clouds, see them for what they are and then find a way to look through them, or to fly higher or lower so we can see past them.

Terry was a senior director in a shipping company who provided tracking solutions that enabled depots to keep watch on their vehicles. Many of their clients were in the USA and as a result, Terry spent half his life in the UK following up sales leads and the other half in the USA keeping track of the sales team there. However, over time the US sales team began to fall behind its target and he was asked by the CEO to manage them more closely. The CEO also fancied himself as a global sales manager and liked to travel to the USA, which meant that the organisation often had two of their top team members in America at the same time, both doing sales work and based in the same office.

If you had been coaching Terry, what would you have noticed happening here? What did he need to pay attention to?

Well, it was obvious that the CEO was checking up on his performance, while simultaneously sabotaging his ability to lead the team. A classic double hit, in my experience. With support, Terry finally began to see the true picture for himself and realised that the organisation didn't need two people flying round the world to the same meetings to do the same job.

With this in mind we started to plan possible career moves, either sideways or outwards, and to model scenarios and rehearse potential conversations, so Terry would be better prepared and could take care of himself. In the end he left the business after a tense but polite 'career discussion' with the CEO.

And the moral of the story? Although Terry responded well to the situation in the end, he could have put more effort into maintaining his awareness in the first place, because once it began to wane, he was a on a gentle slippery slope that ultimately led him out of the business.

SO WHAT?

Put simply, a pilot who lacks awareness is a dead pilot. The risk of a controlled flight into the ground or a violent crash as we lose our sense of direction is too great. We need to be mindful of both our environment and our performance at work every day.

If our environment isn't great then our work will suffer. In addition, if we don't notice our environment we might walk past interesting opportunities or miss vital organisational news.

If we are fatigued or stressed our work will suffer, which of course can lead to a fatal spiral. When our work suffers we get more stressed trying to put it right, which soaks up even more energy, which in turn leaves us with less energy to do the work, that leads to performance issues and then... more stress.

So when we ask 'so what?' we need to take a long slow look at our awareness and be honest with ourselves. Do we want to be successful, or get hurt?

LEARNING EXERCISE

1. Look back at all the antidotes that have been listed in this chapter. Don't worry about remembering them all... the skill is to notice what jumps out at you and to concentrate on those. Our subconscious is very good at guiding us and we can trust our intuition to help us make a good choice.
2. Write down here any three antidotes that particularly appeal to you as practical steps you can take to improve your level of awareness:
   i.
   ii.
   iii.
3. Finally, talk to your partner or your line manager and discuss with them a change you can make to ensure that your awareness doesn't slip. Perhaps you might change the office layout, buy a new diary or a whiteboard to capture notes, hold regular one-to-one performance meetings, or simply go to bed early.

   Write down here the change you wish to talk about:

   _____

   _____

   _____

6
How to Choose Careers
– Navigation Lessons –

COCKPIT QUESTION:
How can you learn to trust your intuition?

IN THE BEGINNING

When you were younger, how often did you experience the classic scenario described below? For illustration, the cast here includes a kindly old aunt, but she's just a cipher for any older well-meaning, and yet slightly annoying, relative or friend of the family…

Aunt: Hello Richard, how are you today?

Me: I'm well, thank you Auntie. How are you?

Aunt: I'm fine too, thank you. *(Pleasantries over, she moves in for the kill).* And tell me Richard, what would like to do when you grow up?

Me: *(Earnestly)* Well Auntie, I'd like to be a pilot.

Aunt: Ooh that's nice dear. I think you'd look smart in a uniform.

Me: (*Thinks… Hmmmph, we'll see. Can I go now, you daft old bat?*)

This story has a couple of alternative answers from me:

Option (A)

Aunt: Tell me Richard, what would like to do when you grow up?

Me: Grow up? Are you kidding! Why do I want to grow up?!

Option (B)

Aunt: Tell me Richard, what would like to do when you grow up?

Me: How am I supposed to know?! I'm only eight! The only jobs I've had so far are washing the dishes and annoying my sister, and that latter was less of a job and more of a vocation!

I'm sure you get the picture. At an early age we are asked an impossible question, with no idea of what the mysterious world of work looks like. We may have been lucky and had a thoughtful parent take us to their place of work, keen to show us where they went when we were at school. Or we might have been as clueless as the majority and had very little idea about 'a career'.

The point is this; it's all about learning and it doesn't matter how old we are when we read this chapter, we can all think about what we want to be doing for our career and we don't have to give aged aunts a snap answer. We can take time to think about ourselves and our needs and find a way to meet them.

CAREER? JOB? LIFE? VOCATION?

If a career is the span of our working life, we need to think about the individual roles that it comprises. For some people, this is an easy decision because they find themselves drawn to a particular vocation and make that their life's work. Others have a particular skill set that lends itself to an obvious role, while many are keen to go into the family business or take the advice and guidance of their elders or their teachers. Whatever you are drawn to, it's good to remember that:

- We can choose our path.
- We can make a good enough decision for today.
- We can change direction in the future.

CAREER DECISION SHORTCUT

There is a way to find out what we want to do with our life and happily skip over the rest of this chapter. *We can use our intuition.*

CAREER TOP TIP

Trust your intuition!
(It knows you better than you do.)

Intuition is the unspoken force of thought that lurks deep inside us. It helps us to choose new shoes when we're out shopping or a partner when we're out clubbing, and it generally watches over us and keeps us safe and healthy. If we think about all the decisions we made during the course of one day, we can see that some of them required a bit of thought and that others happened without bothering our conscious mind. When we were getting ready for work that tie 'felt right' or 'that blouse was the one we felt like wearing today' – we all use these phrases that show our intuition is at work.

HOW TO USE YOUR INTUITION

We can tap into our intuition by noticing things we are drawn to. It's a bit like choosing clothes – we can often say a bit about why we like something, but aren't able to articulate the *exact* reasons why beyond 'I just like it'.

Career choices can be the same and to say 'I know all the arguments and I just want to do it' is a really helpful way to give our intuition an outlet. It can also be useful to think about the following questions in our search for direction:

ACCESSING INTUITION

Q1) What areas of work do you feel drawn to?
Q2) Who do you secretly admire and wish you had their job?[7]
Q3) Which jobs leave you feeling cold when someone suggests them to you?
Q4) What roles do you find yourself researching over and over again?

The third question is designed to box off particular areas of interest, because it helps to narrow our thinking by disregarding areas that we know we do not want. The other questions pick up on our habits of constantly filtering information to see whether it fits with our needs and desires. We are drawn to certain areas

---

[7] This is my favourite question, because for me it cuts right to the heart of the matter. We can use our feelings to guide us and a little friendly envy can be a good clue to the shape of our thinking.

and will naturally explore them, ask questions, volunteer time and generally begin to make things happen. If we make ourselves aware of what we are drawn to, we can use that information to steer our rocket along a career arc that satisfies us.

CASE STUDY – RICHARD

I'm using myself as a case study, not to be smart, but because the experiences surprised me. Fifteen years ago I was back at university, having great fun on a post-graduate programme, learning how to run businesses and save money by improving production processes. It was interesting and challenging work and yet somehow it was a bit unsatisfying to me and the thought of spending the rest of my life as a factory manager seemed like a dismal prospect.

I'd started the course because it fitted with my previous experience and was a route out of junior management into a more serious role. Within a week, two things happened. The first was that we had an inspirational marketing lecture about the simplicity and relevance of business to business marketing. I was hooked and assumed everyone else would be too, only to find that the rest of my intake had enjoyed the day but hadn't been particularly bowled over. I'd always been a bit sceptical of marketing professionals on account of having met some arrogant marketers who were a poor advert for their industry. The lecture changed my view.

Later that week, we had a new lecture by someone who called themselves a 'business coach' and it was the first time

I had come across the term. What struck me during their talk was that coaching enabled them to deploy thinking skills, gave them a varied workload across many different businesses and that the person was talking about it with such passion and enthusiasm, it was clearly an exciting and rewarding job to do.

I didn't know anything about the realities of working as a coach or delivering marketing solutions, but my interest was hooked and I knew I wanted my career to include these new disciplines. At the end of the course I secured a job as a business development manager, that combined marketing with process improvement, and when that had run its course and I'd had fun as a General Manager, I changed direction and set up my own business as a development coach and leadership specialist. Along the way I added writing, speaking and radio-hosting to my week and now have a portfolio of work that I love as much on day 3,650 as I did on day 1.

All that success grew from noticing what had struck me by surprise during two days of my life. At the time I didn't know how to use marketing in a job or how to make a start as a coach, but I knew I really wanted to find out!

CAREER CHOICE PERMISSIONS

What made my career path successful was that, without realising it at the time, I had given myself internal *permission* to follow what interested me. I was on the university programme to become a factory manager or a change agent, and while these two options were interesting, I had a sense they would be stifling too (based on previous factory experience). I was on the course because it was the best length of rope I had to climb out from my current level and up to something more exciting, but that didn't mean that I couldn't adjust my direction of travel slightly to end up three steps to the left of the landing point that had been planned for me.

Permissions are powerful. They are the force that adjusts the levers in the 'signal box of control' in our head, allowing new thoughts to flow and new actions to follow. We can be given these permissions by friends and people who influence us, we can read them and we can give them to ourselves. Often the most powerful ones are absorbed when someone confounds us – perhaps a manager who we thought didn't like us much takes us to one side and suggests we go for that promotion because we have real talent. The unexpectedness of it means that our usual defences of disbelief and self-deprecation are down. Instead of the permission bouncing off the tough skin that shields us from the world it zooms right in, lands deeply and – click – a change happens inside us.

Think about permissions for a moment. When did someone change your view or encourage you onward with thoughtful words of support?

Positive permissions can make a life-changing difference. We can *give ourselves permission* to take the permissions we need to have the career which we want to. Have a look at the following list of permissions and see which ones jump out at you. You can choose one, or some, or take one that isn't quite right for you and change the words to make it fit snugly.

CAREER CHOICE PERMISSIONS

These are all true statements. Which ones jump out at you as you read them? Take them – they're yours and they will make a useful difference to you.

1. We can take time to choose our career path.
2. We can be inspired by people, place, subject, style, complexity, challenge, content and choice.
3. We can make our own decisions.
4. We can listen to others and can decide what to do with their words.
5. We do not have to follow our parents – we can choose for ourselves.
6. We can learn new skills.
7. We can learn from our experience.
8. We can learn from other people's experience.
9. We can find out the facts.
10. We can match our skills to suitable roles and create a shortlist of opportunities.
11. We can trust our intuition.
12. We can follow our heart.
13. We can decide on our priorities for life.
14. We can have needs and wants.
15. We can get our needs and wants met.
16. We can make course changes.
17. We can retrain.

18. We can be resourceful and get help from friends or professionals.
19. We can do something we love.
20. We can find combinations that work for us.
21. We can take a break and start again, or start differently.
22. We can change our path as we grow and learn.
23. We can enjoy finding out and exploring.
24. We can love something for what it is, without analysis or explanation.
25. We can know that having our career does not make us 'selfish', it means we are leading our own life and not someone else's life.

I've worked with people across the world and enabled them to make progress with their career, get started again after a falter, reach the next level or make a complete change. In many cases, people have a strong sense of what they would like to do and all they need is a friendly, honest and truthful permission to enable them to take the first step. We can have fun practicing with permissions by offering them to friends, partners, children and colleagues. They're meant to be shared, because they enable people to grow their career.

EXERCISE 1 – JOB GRID

Here is practical way to put our intuition and our new permissions to good use. On page 111 is a grid that comprises 99 jobs and one blank square. Here's the exercise:

- Scan the grid for 5 seconds and circle two roles which appeal to you.

- Then scan the grid again for another 5 seconds and at the end circle another two roles that appeal to you.
- Finally, scan the grid a third time but instead of circling any roles, write a role into the blank square. This can be one you've seen or one that has come into your mind.

This will give you five possibilities and you'll have used your intuition to narrow down the grid to the 5% that really interests you. It doesn't matter if you like the sound of a job without knowing much about it – we can always spend time on research later. Every day we read newspapers, listen to the news, interact with people and notice the world around us, so we are constantly soaking up information about people and their roles. We have a rough idea of what it's like to do hundreds of different jobs because we've seen people doing their work, spoken with them, hired them or purchased goods and services from them.

Therefore, it is okay to look at the job grid and let our intuition guide us, because we have all this information logged in our databank.

Write down the five roles that interest you in the box on page 112. This is a starting point and you're welcome to change them or add to them.

JOB GRID

Researcher	Cook	Assembler	Vet	Traveller	Painter	Fisherman	Producer	Model	
Engineer	Footballer	Social Worker	Pilot	Carpenter	Director	Officer	Host	Singer	Builder
Programmer	Athlete	Campaigner	Designer	Firefighter	Cleaner	Celebrity	Scientist	Owner	Designer
Nurse	Priest	Adventurer	Coach	Waiter	Politician	Networker	Soldier	Lecturer	Supervisor
Postman	Entrepreneur	Salesperson	Agent	Linguist	Plumber	Journalist	Receptionist	Operative	Mechanic
Farmer	Lawyer	Historian	Sailor	Photographer	Administrator	Supervisor	Critic	Accountant	Sculptor
Writer	Buyer	Planner	Dancer	Caregiver	Rescuer	Shop Assistant	Actor	Driver	Clerk
Commander	Potter	Healer	Teacher	Musician	Zookeeper	Doctor	Daredevil	Youth Worker	Curator
Mentor	Policeman	Paramedic	Tailor	Architect	Consultant	Fitness Instructor	Scholar	Promoter	Marketer
Stylist	Hotelier	Chef	Creator	Editor	Inventor	Artist	Comedian	Trader	Advisor

MY INTUITION CHOSE THESES FIVE ROLES FOR ME TO THINK ABOUT:
1.
2.
3.
4.
5.

EXERCISE 2 – SKILLS & APTITUDES

Once we have a selection of possible job roles, we can think about our skills and aptitudes more closely. We can tap into our intuition again to remind ourselves what we're naturally good at. These are not about which areas we have to work hard at, but what we're *naturally* able to do.

Here is the exercise:

- Read the table on the next page, taking 30 seconds to consider all 80 boxes.
- Choose four attributes that you consider to be your primary strengths – things that come relatively easy to you.
- Scan the boxes for another 10 seconds and choose four that could be secondary strengths.
- Finally, chose one wild card that appeals to you. The wild card is a skill which you can exhibit if you're particularly focussed, diligent or under pressure.

This will give you 9 items of interest.

SKILLS & ATTRIBUTES GRID

Prefers exercise to sitting	Proactive	Exudes warmth	Accepts direction	Works well alone	Enjoys competition	Organised	Authoritative	Reads maps	Politically astute
Enjoys new things	Ambitious	Public speaking	Collaborates	Walking	Facility for language	Thinks deeply	Witty	Caring for others	Follows rules
Assertive	Notices others	Punctual	Finds out information	Can see patterns	Intuitive	Diligent	Calm	Dedicated	Takes measured risks
Reliable	Team player	Animal husbandry	Creative	Neat and tidy	Complex mathematics	Polite	Plans thoroughly	Embraces change	Is listened to
Good in a crisis	Working with hands	Likes the outdoors	Good at learning	Seeks challenges	Patient	Problem solver	Talking	Practical	Can remember theories
Resourceful	Engages people	Playful	Reading	Sells ideas	Strong sense of spatial awareness	Writing	Inventive	Reactive	Careful
Enjoys detail	Can draw	Confident with arithmetic	Presenting	Builds consensus	Can follow orders	Always completes tasks	Analysis and deduction	Listens	Accepts other points of view
Good at fixing things	Leads from the front	Explores	Creates solutions	Smiles	Has a flexible outlook	Independent	Works at speed	Works well under pressure	Lively

Please write down your four primary skills, your four secondary skills and one wild card skill in the box below. You're welcome to add more if there is another skill or attribute that you really must have on the list. The purpose of inviting us to focus is that our tendency is to collect a big basket of positives, which can lead us in so many directions that we end up going nowhere. The more we hone our thinking to a sharp point, the clearer our direction will be.

MY PRIMARY SKILLS INCLUDE:
1.
2.
3.
4.
MY SECONDARY SKILLS INCLUDE:
5.
6.
7.
8.
MY WILD CARD IS:

Remember that we can learn technical skills such as report writing or presentation skills. There is also a difference between being able to write a report and being someone who loves to play with language and who finds writing a deeply satisfying task. The former attribute is part of a role, whereas the latter is suitable to form the core of a role.

EXERCISE 3 – MATCHING & COMPARING

We now have a reasonable sense of the kind of roles we are interested in and our own natural skills and attributes. It's tempting to argue that we have more than nine key skills and although some people are talented polymaths, the majority of us use three or four core skills that tend to come naturally and flow readily. If we use these in our role then we will perform to a higher standard, operate under less stress, have the capacity to learn new techniques and can apply nuances in skilful ways that add value.

Conversely, if we do our best to shoehorn ourselves into a career path that ignores our skills, we could be setting ourselves up for low performance, failure and even hardship. Piloting a rocket is hard enough without deliberately flying it into the eye of the storm. It makes more sense and is better for our long-term health and well-being if we make life easy for us and play to our strengths.

Here is the matching and comparing exercise:

- Please transfer your answers from Exercise 1 and Exercise 2 into the boxes on the following page, then pause and take a long look at them, before answering the following questions:

  Q1. What do you notice?

  Q2. Which skills appear to fit with which roles?

  Q3. Which roles do you need to find out more information about?

Q4. Which skill or attribute do you feel is central to a fulfilling career for you?

Q5. What skills, attributes or roles are missing from the list?

Q6. What are you thinking now?

MATCHING & COMPARING	
My intuition chose these five roles for me to think about:	My Primary Skills include:
1.	1.
2.	2.
3.	3.
4.	4.
5.	My Secondary Skills include:
When I compare these roles with my skills and attributes, what do I notice?	5.
	6.
	7.
	8.
	My Wild Card is:

In our career, we may move between several different roles and enjoy many different levels of seniority. As with all good decisions, the key to success is to take time for quality thinking and to add a dash of realism to the cocktail of our dreams and aspirations. Working life can be tough, in terms of getting and keeping a job, and yet employers will always comment that:

- Good people are hard to find.
- They tend to retain good people.

If we build a career out of roles which allow us to demonstrate our natural talents and abilities, we will increase the chance of being considered a 'good person', thus making it easier for people to hire us and more likely that they will keep us.[8]

EXERCISE 4 – CAREER DYNAMICS

Now that we have a sense of what roles we might be interested in and the key skills we can bring to them, we can consider some of the more dynamic aspects of our career – namely the characteristics that shape different roles. For example, you may have considered a career as a shop assistant or a manager and yet these roles are very different if you're in a commercial organisation versus a not-for-profit organisation. They're also really different if you have to work shifts, or work a regular 9-to-5 week.

Here is the exercise:

- Below is a set of typical job-related scales for us to think about.
- For each item, we can put a cross on the line next to the box with our preferred career choices.
- In some cases, such as working abroad, we may only choose this for a short time, in order to gain experience so that we can return home on a promotion.

---

[8]   A 'good person' doesn't mean that we are dull or lifeless. We can be talented and display warmth and humour, have fun and sometimes party. It's all about playing to our strengths.

CAREER TOP TIP

We may have to go away to work,
to get the experience we need,
to come home to a bigger and better role.

Career Dynamics Exercise – On each line, put a cross closest to the box that best fits your career/role preferences.

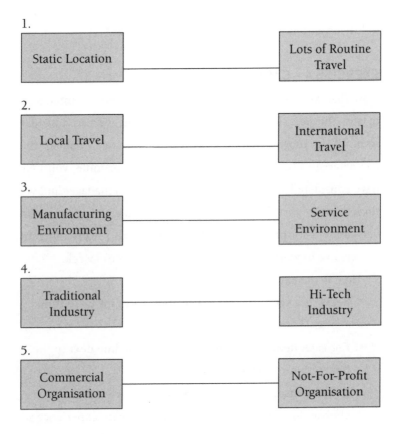

1.

| Static Location | Lots of Routine Travel |

2.

| Local Travel | International Travel |

3.

| Manufacturing Environment | Service Environment |

4.

| Traditional Industry | Hi-Tech Industry |

5.

| Commercial Organisation | Not-For-Profit Organisation |

6.

| Large Organisation | —————— | Small Organisation |

7.

| Owned by Shareholders | —————— | Owned by One Family |

8.

| Fast-paced Environment | —————— | Slower-paced Environment |

9.

| Rapidly-Changing Environment | —————— | Static Environment |

10.

| Promotion Through Time Served | —————— | Promotion by Ability |

11.

| High Freedom to Act | —————— | Follow Set Procedures |

12.

| Work with People | —————— | Work with Tasks |

13.

| Detailed, Careful Work | —————— | Simpler, General Tasks |

14.

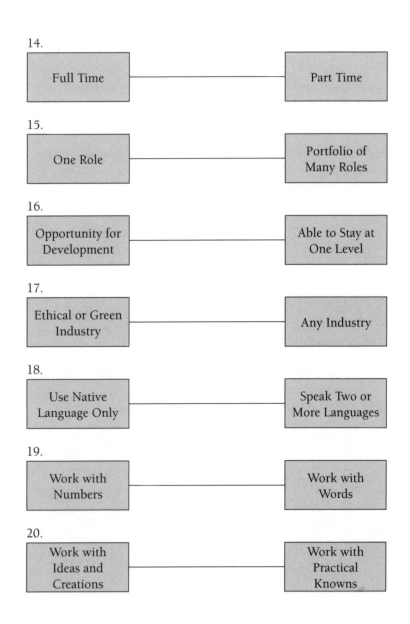

| Full Time | | Part Time |

15.

| One Role | | Portfolio of Many Roles |

16.

| Opportunity for Development | | Able to Stay at One Level |

17.

| Ethical or Green Industry | | Any Industry |

18.

| Use Native Language Only | | Speak Two or More Languages |

19.

| Work with Numbers | | Work with Words |

20.

| Work with Ideas and Creations | | Work with Practical Knowns |

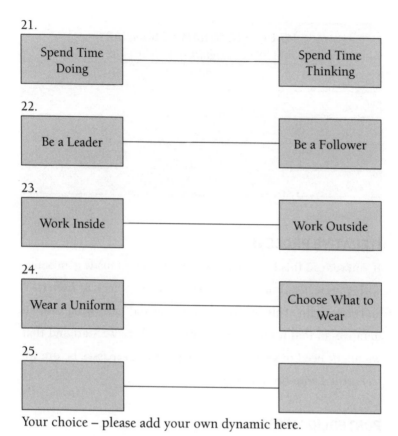

21.

Spend Time Doing — Spend Time Thinking

22.

Be a Leader — Be a Follower

23.

Work Inside — Work Outside

24.

Wear a Uniform — Choose What to Wear

25.

Your choice – please add your own dynamic here.

This exercise gives us a general sense of what we're interested in and helps to broaden our thinking so that we can check the roles and skills against the environment we would like to locate them in. To capture the essence of our preferences, we can choose five items that are the most important to use and write them here, so they stand out from the crowd:

MY CAREER DYNAMICS SUMMARY *Five areas of significance to me are:*	
1.	
2.	
3.	
4.	
5.	

ITERATIVE PROCESS

If you've read this far and are wondering if you made a 'mistake' with any earlier choices you're welcome to go back to *Exercise 1* and start again. This process of thinking and narrowing is often iterative, in that it doesn't really matter where we start and that we might need to go round the loop for a few passes before we feel settled with our answers.

PORTFOLIO LIFESTYLE

We encountered this concept in my case study earlier, where I had built a portfolio of different income and activity streams. In essence, it means having several smaller eggs in your basket rather than one large egg. I've learnt that I love working with people in organisations and that I'm better when visiting them, instead of having a permanent desk in the corner of the office. That's my style and it took a few years to figure that out. It doesn't mean people with one egg are missing out – the litmus test is if we're happy. That's really all that matters. With the advent of micro-jobs, where people work for 10 hours a week in return for lower tax rates, it's likely that people will combine three or more different jobs to make up a full week's salary. Many of us essentially already have a portfolio career – we might be a manager, a craftsman, a wife, a parent, a school governor and a member of sporting team or leisure club.

There is also no truth that a portfolio working life earns you more money or is more recession proof. What matters here is the amount of money we need to keep our home and health together and if we lose a quarter of our income, that can mean a slow spiral into debt. Losing one job is difficult and yet also frees us up to look for our next role. There is no optimum combination, we can do what works for us and enjoy it for what it is.

PUTTING IT ALL TOGETHER – THE CAREER SCOPE

This chapter has pulled together the four major elements of career choice:

- Roles
- Skills
- Comparison
- Dynamics

Now that we have a clearer sense of what career we would like to have (which may be different from where we currently are) we can pull all the strands together to create a unified picture, which we can call a *career-scope*. To create your own career-scope, go back through the exercises in this chapter and transfer your answers into the relevant section of the diagram below, so that you can see all of your responses in one place. For example, when considering career dynamics you can write in the words that best fit your choices from earlier, such as 'inside', 'practical', 'service environment' and so on.

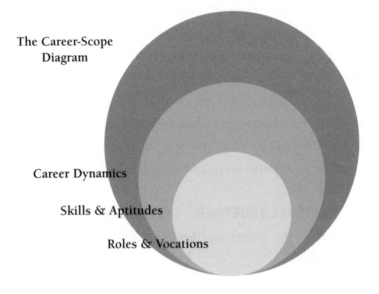

The Career-Scope Diagram

Career Dynamics

Skills & Aptitudes

Roles & Vocations

REFLECTION TIME

Defining a career and making choices isn't about complete objectivity, because that is almost impossible to achieve given that we're an exciting mix of thoughts, feelings, assumptions and our own sense of internal logic. Therefore, our aim is for 'thoughtful subjectivity' where we temper our natural likes and dislikes with reasonable amounts of information and cross-checking. Look again at your completed career-scope and notice the words you've written. Pay attention to:

- Patterns.
- Areas of natural affinity.
- Items that don't really fit together.
- Things that surprise you (perhaps because they're on the diagram or missing from it).
- The new thoughts, questions and decisions that you begin to form as a result of your reflection.

SO WHAT?

Our career is our affair – we have one life and one chance to fly our rocket in the direction that we wish to travel. We might make course corrections, even pull hard on the control column and cause a radical shift, and all of that is okay within the scope of a modern career.

If this chapter has raised more questions for you than answers, that suggests you're thinking about your life and what you're doing with it and that can only be a good thing. It might mean that we need to hire the services of a professional coach and/ or a counsellor and share our thinking with someone who can scrutinise our plans and ambitions and encourage us in a friendly yet determined manner. If we can provide them with answers and notice ourselves digging deep to justify our direction then good for us – that tends to show we are genuinely committed at a deeper level and thus stand a greater chance of success.

However, if we're not that interested in fighting our corner and don't really have the heart for a bit of honest 'push back', then we need to ask ourselves if we really have what it takes to achieve what we *say* we want. For example, I've met plenty of people who have said that they'd like to have my job as a coach and writer, own their own business and build a portfolio career and yet I've met very few who have wanted to spend £20,000 retraining themselves, wanted to work 18-hour days and weekends, find and enlist the help of five supporters, be prepared to learn sales skills and then have a roller-coaster ride of budgets, unpredictable working patterns and the need to be your own managing director, chief buyer, debt collector and tea maker.

As I say to everyone I work with when supporting them to make career choices and find the direction they want to go in:

> **IF** you want it – you can have it.
>
> **AND** you've got to be prepared to pay for it!

LEARNING EXERCISE

1. Look back at all the permissions from earlier in the chapter and write down three of them that really struck a chord with you here:
   i)
   ii)
   iii)
2. Now look again at the career-scope you completed and answer this question: What do I conclude from this diagram?

   _____

   _____

   _____

7

Setting Career Goals

– Money vs. Happiness –

COCKPIT QUESTION:
What's it all about for you?

A LIFE LIVED

The point of this chapter is to invite us to think more deeply about what is pulling us through our career. Are we following a happy direction of travel, or have we lost our compass and are navigating along a route that feels increasingly uncomfortable?

Goals are good. They give us a point on the horizon to aim for and enable us to make sense of our current situation by relating it to a direction of travel. We need to have a career goal, otherwise we'll have no method of assessing the degree of our success.

IF WE RETIRED NOW...

If we had to retire this minute and not work anymore, what thoughts and feelings fill our mind as we reflect back over our career? How will we judge that it has been a success? Will we count the number of bedrooms in our palace, or the number of friends down at the golf club? Will we celebrate the money we saved by hurting less powerful suppliers, or revel in our image as a hatchet-person, brought in to remove loyal employees at an undignified speed? Have we made a difference to society, supported a talented person to reach their potential, or used our skills to make a tiny contribution towards improving the lives of others?

It's sobering to think about the progress of our rocket and to see if we are on track or have steadily wandered off course, or been consumed by a ruthless ambition that pushed people to one side and diminished our relationships.

Perhaps we have had a brilliant career so far and can pause long enough to open a bottle of champagne and celebrate our success. Brilliant doesn't have to mean wealthy – it means that we are happy with our progress and are following a plan that brings us joy and satisfaction.

SUN-TANNED HAPPINESS IS A MYTH

Given today's proliferation of entertainment media, we could be forgiven for thinking that the world is full of 'celebs' who all live in the sunshine, have 365-day perma-tans, teeth that dazzle and an enviable lifestyle which seems to comprise of mostly chatting about their enviable lifestyle. By contrast, our lives may seem pale and dull, our teeth crooked and our summer tans long forgotten.

Who has the better life?

It's hard to say for sure, but it's a fair bet that we've been duped and the answer is, in most cases, we do. This is because we only see what goes on in front of the camera and we don't see the grind of looking beautiful all the time, having to forgo our privacy, or having every tiny mistake and fresh bulge of fat drooled over in newspapers and websites.

Although a few young people have identified being a WAG (Wives And Girlfriends of rich sportsmen) as a profession (it isn't) and aspire to lead the field in it, that's a fantasy and not always a pleasant one, when you consider how many 'celebrities' seem to have a very stressful media-fuelled life at home.

So when we think about what happiness might be, we need to take a long, cool, appraising look at the stereotypes we see in the media and then throw them away. They're a tiny distorting minority and only serve to blind us to how happy we can be without all of their fake fur and disposable husbands.

DON'T LIVE A LIE

We are all motivated by a basic desire to feed ourselves, find a decent home to live in and to have a life that includes love and friendship and something interesting to do during the daylight hours. Everything else is a bonus.

When we lose our job or we have a period of ill-health, our motivating forces are thrown into sharp relief. It only takes a day of extreme pain to remind us that our health is more important than our smartphone. It only takes a redundancy situation to remind us that our partner really does love us and is far more important than all the hours we spent typing up meeting notes, instead of enjoying the company of our companions.

If our motivation is misguided, we will cause ourselves real heartache and will begin to lead a double life. This happens where we tell our friends and colleagues that we're having a great time, when we secretly we wish to be somewhere else, doing something completely different. However, because we've told everyone how brilliant our life is, we have to stick with the lie or risk sounding like a fool. We are trapped, until we can finally find the courage to share the problems we are facing, or we burn out and our career engine seizes, leaving us to plummet and crash to the ground.

If you're living a lie then be kind to yourself – find a confidential counsellor to talk to and begin to unravel the strings that bind you to a miserable present.

BEWARE THE DAZZLE OF METALLIC PAINT

I had a friend who worked ridiculous hours as a management consultant and who spent every weekend writing reports and catching up on correspondence, so that she could start the following week up-to-date and on top on her workload. Her commitment to her host organisation was beyond question, but you didn't have to look too hard to see past the 5-star hotels and executive dinners to realise that it was a fairly empty life. I asked her once why she worked so hard and her answer was that it allowed her to choose metallic paint as an option on her company car.

I think this is a very sad story. There is nothing wrong in working hard, or having a sporty car to make the miles more fun, but she had started to lose sight of the real world of people and adventure and instead had entered a dark corporate world of work and more work. I once coached a financial specialist in London and asked why he hadn't become a broker and doubled his money.

'Have you seen their lifestyle?' was his tart reply. 'They work 16-hour days and have no time to do anything else but sleep. Sure they get paid double what I do, but most of them are burnt out by the time they're 40 and need the money to fund their recovery.'

It was a sobering conversation. I'm sure there are a few traders who have fun filled days and manage to get out of the office and smell the flowers. And I'm sure there are plenty of people following different careers who are equally locked in to a depressing cycle of work-money-work-money.

Having a house can make us happy. Having a house that is twice the size does not automatically make us twice as happy and if we're working hard simply to acquire more 'things' then we need to pause and take a long, hard look at what life has become for us. Here are three interesting questions to consider:

- Would you rather work 5 days a week and have a large house or work 4 days a week and have a smaller house and indulge in a favourite hobby on the 5th day?
- What would you do on that 5th day?
- What would you like your children to do when they're riding their rockets?

Many people are motivated by money and equate more money with more happiness. This is a pity because life has so much more to offer. Always remember our children look up to us and learn from our words and our actions.

What are you really teaching your children?

A PROFOUND INSIGHT

It was a sunny day and I had popped in to see a colleague in her office. She wasn't available for a few minutes, so to kill time I knocked on her neighbour's door (who I also knew well) and chatted with her instead. After the usual pleasantries, she asked me how life was and I replied that although I could always use an extra client or two, the reality was that I was in a happy place. I had work, a radio show, a book to market and I was neither at the bottom of the pile or racing to reach the top. She smiled warmly, and said:

'That's so good Richard – you're happy in the middle – and that's the best place to be.'

CAREER TOP TIP

The best place to be is… happy in the middle.

HAPPY IN THE MIDDLE

The phrase has stuck with me ever since because there is an essential honesty to it. There will always be someone richer than us, with a bigger house, more employees or a better wine cellar. I've worked with several wealthy people who are often caught up in a financial arms race to make sure they win that deal so they can buy *that* yacht or provide their children with a magnificently expensive private education. We all make life choices and it's okay to be ambitious and to want the best for our families. However, if this becomes a win-at-all-costs mentality then we are pursuing a pointless goal.

Middle doesn't mean mediocrity and we can work hard and flex our talents to be happy bobbing about in the middle. The idea of 'middle' doesn't reflect a work-life balance either, because as I always say, there is no such thing as work-life balance – it's an impossible goal.

ONE GOAL IS IMBALANCE

One career goal to think about is where we want to be on the work-life continuum. Maintaining a balance point between work and play drains energy, so we're much better advised to make life easier for ourselves and aim for a workable *imbalance*. We will tend to work for over 40 hours per week, so the chances of finding 40 hours of leisure time or being able to reduce our working hours to 20 is only a remote possibility. Instead, we can make sure that we have at least two hours of personal time each week. It doesn't matter where that time falls, as long as it's ours to indulge ourselves in, whether we go running, read a book, build a model, play a sport or sit in the bath and gently turn into a contented prune.

We can add to this two-hour slot to give ourselves more time to unwind – two hours *is* the bare minimum though. We have to talk to our children and partners so that they understand we need some space and they can have space too – we do not have to be SuperMum or SuperDad (or SuperWorker) and we can all give ourselves:

- Permission to play.
- Permission to put ourselves first for a while.
- Permission to invest in our free time.
- Permission to enjoy ourselves.
- Permission to take a technology break.

I've consciously included this last permission because I've noticed that we often have a nasty habit of taking time off and taking our smartphone with us so that we can 'keep an eye on it'. Have you been to a Tweet-up (a gathering of people who chat on Twitter) and noticed that after the first couple of drinks have been consumed everyone is on their phone, tweeting away and telling the rest of the world what a great time they're having? I have – it was depressing, so we put the phones away, moved to a quiet corner and chatted amiably.

Having our smartphone with us means that this time could still be considered work, because it's not giving our mind a rest from the wider world. It's the same as spending the weekend playing email-tennis with our work colleagues. We con ourselves into thinking that we are being productive, but in reality we are frittering away valuable personal time when we could instead switch off our phone and give our over-stressed brains a day or two to rest.

We can include fun goals in our career planning and can use these questions to prod our brains into action:

- How good is your imbalance?
- What do you need to talk to your partner about changing?
- What permission do you give yourself?

PARENTS & BIRTH ORDER

Every child grows up with people who raise them and we can class all of these people as 'parents', whatever their biological or social background. These people tend to be well meaning and they encourage us by asking questions and stimulating our interest. They also have a tendency to dump their fears and aspirations on us, which shape our future career ambitions and goals. Perhaps they are senior managers and expect us to reach the same heights as they did. Perhaps they are a devoted doctor and expect us to follow in the footsteps of our dad, granddad and great granddad. Perhaps they tell us not to pursue their trade, or not to become a manager and turn into 'one of the bosses'.

Birth order can make a difference to the message we receive from our parents and to its intensity. The first born starts off as an only child and gets all the attention, all the hope and all the fears. At this point, our parents don't know if they will have more children so they tend to over-invest in us, just in case we are the only vessel to carry their family ambitions out into the world. First-born children tend towards perfectionism as they want to get it right for their parents and they often become leaders and seek responsibility.

The arrival of the next child turns the first child from an only child into an elder child, who now has to learn to share mum and dad and may resent that. Parents are often more relaxed with their second child, because they know how to look after them and that babies are more robust then they first realised. As a consequence they give them more freedom to pursue their own agenda. Second children tend to follow their own path and allow their own desires to guide them.

If a third child comes along the dynamic changes again, with the second child falling into the empty space that is the 'middle child'. They're not the eldest who carries responsibility, nor are they the youngest (who often becomes Daddy's little prince or princess). They can become invisible without a clearly defined role and often fade into the background and rebel and become fiercely independent.

The third child is often over indulged, because they're the baby in the family. This can cause career problems when the person grows up to be too reliant on their parents, or is not allowed to grow up into a mature adult and accept responsibility for themselves in the same way their siblings have had to. Third children may need more support to get a job and may be more reliant on their parents if they take longer to mature into independent adults.

Our parents love us and did the best job that they knew how to with the time, money, resources and background available to them. Our physis – our inner life force – means that we have made a choice whether to accept or reject their messages. We can't wholly blame our parents for our happiness or lack of – we can acknowledge their part in our career goals and, at the same time, remember that we are our own person. We alone are responsible for our choices and actions. Love your parents, but put aside their aspirations for you and make your own career decisions.

WHAT IS YOUR CAREER GOAL?

Although we may have many smaller goals, we often have one central ambition that pulls us towards an end point. We might let ourselves be derailed by following the path our parents chose for us and revisit our dream later in life, or we might work diligently to get where we think we want to go. I use the words 'think we want to go' because until we've reached it we don't know exactly what it will be like. We may arrive and find we're in a good place or realise that the reality of our situation does not match our expectations.

Here are three examples of this reality in action:

- A friend of mine wanted to be a lawyer and once she had been made a partner realised she had no life outside of the office, so she gave it up and moved into marketing.

- A colleague wanted to be a consultant and worked hard to secure a role with an international company, only to find out that he wasn't suited to the politics and pace of the business. What he really wanted to do was to design electronic components and the experience convinced him that he would be better off sticking to his genuine ambition.

- A journalist tired of the long hours and ever-present threat of deadlines. She tapped into her love of organic farming and moved into the sausage business, where she created a profitable and award-winning brand.

A career goal often reflects a specific point that we want to get to. Do you know your career goal? As you are reading this are you wondering what it could be? Or has it changed significantly and you now have a new burning ambition to achieve?

Consider these prompts and ask yourself how they relate to you:

CAREER GOAL PROMPTS

Which ones fit and which ones are you not interested in?

Obtain a university degree.
Secure the top job in your field.
Own your own business.
Become financially independent.
Acquire a specific expertise.
Become known as a world expert.
Campaign for change.
Win a specific award.
Leave your mark on the world.
Work for the good of society.
Found an organisation.
Publish or record something.
Be awarded a medal.
Be happy in the middle.

Notice what your intuition selected from the above list. We all have goals, even if they are sometimes smothered by the need to do our day job. What fuels your ambition? What is your secret wish? What will be the high point of your career? Consider these questions and then write down one career goal, to help you decide what you really want to do.

MY CAREER GOAL
(Is to achieve what by when?)

_____

_____

_____

AND THEN WHAT?

Once you have achieved you goal, what happens next? On Monday your goal is in sight, you achieve it on Thursday and spend Friday enjoying yourself and celebrating. However, what does it feel like on the following Monday? Do you wake up full of energy and keen to start phase two or are you incapacitated by the shock of having nothing to achieve? I raise the question of 'and then what?' for two reasons:

1. If we don't look beyond the achievement of our ambition we could find ourselves waking up to an empty life. It's too late at this point to go back and 'un-sell' the business that we've just sold.

2. Our goal may be something we set out to achieve at a relatively young age and we need to think about what to do after we have won the medal and plan for it accordingly. When we're 20 years old, the idea of reaching our 40th birthday is laughably far away. However, time seems to accelerate with age as the complexity of life increases, so we need to keep setting new goals to keep us focussed into the future.

Always look beyond the end of the line to see what comes next and plan for it. A year before I left my paid role as a manager, I knew I wanted to retrain as a coach and so I began to practice my skills and prepare for the next goal. As it turned out I hadn't practiced nearly enough and had to work hard when I started my business, but thankfully I did have a few experiences to call on when potential clients asked about my coaching background.[9]

SO WHAT?

Where are we flying our rocket to?

What is our career goal?

We can think about what is pulling us towards the future and about whether we are swapping our life for money or for happiness. We can have money and be happy at the same time and we can have money and be utterly miserable. However, if we pursue a career that is ruthlessly focused on money, we could find ourselves setting up our career for a hollow victory. We reach our goal and turn around to find that we've left our family, friends and sense of perspective behind.

Ambition is great, but naked, ruthless, driving ambition can be destructive. This is why it's so helpful to think about being **happy in the middle** – that will enable us to achieve reasonable career goals without destroying ourselves in the process.

---

[9] Nobody wants to be our first client. It's too risky for them, unless their needs are not that complex, or they just take pity on us and decide to help our career with an early purchase order.

LEARNING EXERCISE

Think again about our career goal and the permissions we may need in order to achieve it. Do these permissions align with our goal and support us? Or do we need to get permission from someone else? Write down here what you need to hear and from whom, in order to feel comfortable about following your most cherished career ambition:

_____

_____

_____

8
How To Change Careers
– Pulling G –

G-FORCES CAN BE FATAL

Here's a cheery way to start this chapter – by talking about death. When a pilot pulls back on the control column or banks hard, blood is drawn away from his brain and towards his feet, which can lead to unconsciousness and subsequent death when his now out-of-control jet spins into the ground. This means that in the seconds leading up to the turning point he must prepare himself, by tensing his muscles and ensuring that his G-suit is inflated so it pushes against the increased blood flow to his legs and keeps his brain functioning.

As we are riding the rocket through our career, we need to prepare for any sharp turns that we intend to make, because a lack of preparation can have terrible consequences. This chapter offers a useful checklist of essential items to consider before we make a move.

PRACTICAL EXPERIENCE

I've worked with a wide range of professional managers, technicians and consultants to support them through a career change. One of my colleagues gave up his managing director's post in his own graphics business so that he could start up in web design, and I know a French helicopter pilot who now flies as a civilian contractor in the Far East. People take calculated risks to follow their heart and make profound career changes every day. This chapter is based on first-hand practical experience of what works and what we need to do to change careers.

A RECESSION MAKES IT MORE DIFFICULT

In 2008/9, the USA was hit by the sub-prime mortgage scandal which resulted in massive over-lending to people who couldn't afford the repayments. The country's financial system turned from dependable granite into melted Swiss cheese, banks went bust and people lost their homes. Europe also suffered as the financial volatility triggered a wave of sub-scandals across the Atlantic, with bankers committing sales fraud and exchange rate rigging on a scale that made petty theft seem like a pleasant walk in the park.

The job market froze because companies were either collapsing, waiting to collapse or building up their working capital so that they didn't collapse. The world didn't completely grind to a halt – there were a *few* jobs advertised, but with perhaps 20 excellent applicants for each post only the top of the cream was being skimmed off and the rest were left to struggle. This meant that it was almost impossible to change careers, unless you were thinking about setting up your own business, which is relatively easy to do. The downside of this was the competition from thousands of people who had the same idea.

The point of reminding us about this terrible recession is that it is more difficult to change roles in tumultuous times, when rising unemployment allows organisations to cherry-pick the people with the best skills and experience. There are occasions when we need to sit tight and focus on keeping the job we have – timing is everything.

Take a look at your local economic environment. If it's in recession then don't worry about this chapter for now and revisit it in a few months when things have calmed down. If it's a *mature* recession, when life is starting to go back to normal, or if the economy is growing steadily, then there will be opportunities to change careers and you can read on. A mature recession is one that has been running for more than 12 months, which means organisations have gone through one budget cycle and are starting to recover from the immediate shock of the recession. In career-change terms, this means they realise that even in a recession there is a staff turnover rate and having protected the bank account for a year, it's now possible to relax a little and hire a few new people.

REALITY CHECK

Although career changes can come in a variety of shapes and sizes, the most common two options that we face are swapping an old role for a new one or moving into a different industry, perhaps from public service into the commercial sector. These two options give rise to the Career Step-Change model, as shown below:

The Career Step Change Model

Step Height of 0	Step Height of 1	Step Height of 3	Step Height of 7
NO CHANGE	ACHIEVABLE Requires Perseverance	ACHIEVABLE Requires application and training	ACHIEVABLE Requires application, training, networking and perseverance
Same Role Same Industry 1	Same Role New Industry 2	New Role Same Industry 3	New Role New Industry 4

The model invites us to think about the degree of complexity associated with the career change that we wish to make. It's stepped because it's easier to make a complete switch by first changing either our industry or our skills. If we decide to change *everything* at once, we really need to take a good long look at ourselves, our bank balance and the available goodwill from our family. This is why the step size increases from zero on the left side of the model, to seven on the right. It reflects an increasing scale of difficulty and shows how relatively tricky it is to change both elements in one jump. Sacrifices will have to be made to achieve our goal and we need to ask ourselves:

- How much are we prepared to spend to get where we want to go?
- What support do we need from our loved ones?
- Do we *really* want this change?

CAREER TOP TIP

Reduce risk by changing one thing at a time.

For example, if we want to go from being a doctor's receptionist to a hotel manager, it would make sense to move across to the right industry as a hotel receptionist first, before moving up the management ranks to the right job.

SAME ROLE, NEW INDUSTRY

The easiest move for us is to seek a similar role within a different industry as it allows us to bring most of our skills and experience into play. Although we might be unfamiliar with a few technical terms and particular industry idiosyncrasies, we have enough transferable skills to do the work and enough experience to convince a recruiter that we will add value to their organisation.

- To help bridge the gap, we need exposure to our new industry. We can organise site visits, work as an intern, visit exhibitions, read journals or invite an industry professional to be one of our supporters. This means that when we're asked about our career change, we can talk about our chosen industry with obvious enthusiasm.

NEW ROLE, SAME INDUSTRY

Attempting to stay within our industry and move to a new role is much harder, because our role-specific skills don't count for so much and we have to rely more on our transferable skills. Transferrable skills are the general areas of expertise which are used in many roles and can be easily overlooked because we use them every day and neglect to name them as such. They include our expertise at:

- Planning
- Time management
- Communications
- Resolving conflict
- Problem solving
- Leadership
- Research
- Report writing
- Financial management
- Assertiveness
- Business presentations
- Selling ideas

- Building rapport
- Creativity
- Process improvement

Which ones on this list do you consider to be your key transferrable skills? What is missing from the list that applies to you? It's good to know what we're good at, because we have a wide range of skills, and in my experience, people generally overlook them and omit them from their CV.

To acquire a new role we may need to undergo new training. This may require us to be proactive and complete the training before we get the job, or we may need to volunteer our services for free (or at low cost) to build up experience without costing our host much money (which makes it much easier for them to say yes to us).

Transferrable skills are great, but they often won't be enough to convince an employer that we have what it takes, particularly if we are up against an experienced competitor. To help bridge the gap:

- Talk to someone in the type of role you're interested in and ask them about their qualifications, and more importantly, which areas are most and least useful to them. Then enrole in a course with a high degree of *applied* learning built into it. Experience of application often sells well at an interview because it proves you know what you're doing. If you're going to undertake further education, be practical and think about how well you will fare in an interview if you only know the theory and came up against a candidate who has completed an industrial placement. Experience reduces risk, even if it's only a couple of weeks – it all counts.

NEW ROLE, NEW INDUSTRY

It's possible to make a change and switch both our industry and role at the same time. I've done it myself – twice[10] – and on both occasions it required an investment in training, a small team of professional supporters, a temporary loss of income while I repositioned myself and the ability to take a calculated risk. None of this is easy and it requires us to be genuinely passionate about the role that we're moving towards, because that deep emotional commitment will keep our forward momentum going, even when times get hard and the road ahead seems full of potholes. Recruitment tends to be a risk-averse business because people are expensive to employ, so it's up to us to have great answers to all the killer questions[11] they could ask us at an interview, such as:

- What makes you think you could do this role?
- How can you add value?
- How will you convince other people to take you seriously?
- What will you do to bridge any knowledge gaps that you may have?
- Why should I hire you in preference to someone who has five years of direct experience?

With determination and a willingness to learn, we can change

[10]   From a factory planner to a business development manager, moving from the print industry to the packaging industry. Then a leadership trainer and executive coach in service industries and higher education.

[11]   A killer question is one that causes us to fail the interview because it exposes our fatal weakness. To answer these questions we must be honest and play to our strengths, build solid rapport and share our passion and our commitment. For more information, see the book *Job Hunting 3.0*.

both our roles and industries. We can celebrate our transferrable skills and combine them with new trade and professional skills to strengthen our CV. We can make opportunities for ourselves and we can find ways to bridge the gap between where we are and where we want to be. One great way to bridge the gap is to spend time networking.

NETWORKING

Whenever I'm asked the secret to successful career change, my answer usually comprises two words – *passion* and *networking*. Passion is an overused word that is often uttered by people who think that simply *saying* the word is enough, without substantiating it with evidence of their energy and enthusiasm. If we have a genuine passion for a subject or a task, then we will put in the extra effort for it, make it sparkle for us and will enjoy all aspects of it.

Networking, on the other hand, is an essential discipline to embrace and yet is often not something you'll hear many people claiming to be passionate about. With the rise of social media, however, it could be argued that we're all networkers now and for the purposes of changing our careers we need to be more focused than merely chatting with new friends.

Purposeful networking means making connections with people who could help us to get where we need to go. This is particularly important when we're looking to change careers, because our CV won't always be good enough to go head-to-head with competitors if we simply respond to a job advert.

Networking helps us to solve this problem because people get to know us, and when they do that, they are much more likely to recommend us to a friend or take a chance on us themselves.

HOW TO NETWORK

Many people think networking is about trying to sell people a product, but this is bad form if we do it blatantly and will not win us any prizes. Instead we can meet people, chat with them, share stories and generally get to know them. No selling. Just talking and being friendly. We can then arrange for a second meeting, which is a good time to be more specific about what we're looking for, but don't underestimate the need to find a friend first. People buy from and help people they trust and they don't trust people who shove a CV under their nose and ask directly if they have a job for them.

The best way to network and build a relationship is to follow this simple four-step approach:

4 STEPS OF SUCCESSFUL NETWORKING
Meet – Ask – Connect – Ask

1. **Meet People Face to Face.** Although I'm a big fan of social media, there is still a place for meeting face to face, where we can smile, shake hands and size each other up. We can make a list of all the people we know who could help us – our supporters, local networking groups, friends and colleagues. Then we can arrange to meet them. We only need 30 minutes of their time to make new connections with them.

2. **Ask Questions.** If we want to get to know people then we need to ask them questions to get them talking and then *listen* to the answers. Listening means just that and not waiting for them to draw breath, so we can pounce and talk about ourselves. People feel good about themselves when they're talking and when they're being listened to, and this means they will begin to feel good about us as a result. Questions to ask include:
   - Tell me about yourself?
   - What do you do when you're not working?
   - What do you love about your job, or industry?
   - What trends do you notice in your line of work?
   - How do you find networking?
   - What are *you* looking for?
   - What tips could you offer me?

   These are open questions, which mean they invite the other person to offer us information, which we can then use to ask supplementary questions. The conversation will flow more easily if we're interested in the person and have a smile on our face when conversing. We might be able to help them and reciprocity in a relationship is a great way to develop mutual respect.

3. **Connecting counts.** If networking is a secret of success then connecting with people is the secret within the secret. We are all 'tribal' and belong to various groups, such as being a parent, supporting a particular sports team, where we live, where we shop or take holidays – the list of tribes is endless. We tend to feel more positively disposed towards another person from the same tribe, and when this happens, we connect. To make a connection, all we need to do is to notice when the other person talks about something we have in common. For example, if we ask a networking friend what they like to drink and they wax lyrical about their favourite Bordeaux wine (that we too like to drink), we need to notice this and exclaim, 'Great stuff! I like that too!' The more connections we build, the more we bond with the other person, and will have turned a stranger into a friend.

4. **Ask for Something.** It's okay for us to want things and to be ambitious. We are networking with purpose and it's okay to be nervous and still have a career goal in mind. When we're networking, it's likely that the other person will ask us what we're looking for and if we don't tell them, we won't get anywhere. However, it's good sense to rehearse our answer so we can say the right thing at the critical time. Here are some examples to get us thinking about what we might say:

   Thank you for asking…
   - I'm interested in retraining as a physiotherapist and wondered if you might know someone who I could talk to?
   - I'm currently retraining to be a website designer and I'm looking to increase my practical work experience. Do you know someone who may need to update their website, or would benefit from a spare pair of hands?
   - I'm in transition from a sales manager to a business development coach and I'm looking to meet managing directors and talk with them about helping them to earn more money. Do you know someone whom I could talk to, or network with?

This last question is based on the words I used over 10 years ago to start my business. I was nervous at first and felt a bit of a fraud (many people do on day one, that's really common), but I persevered. The second person whom I spoke with recommended me to the owner of a training company, who in turn introduced me to a valuable client. Notice that by asking 'do you know someone who I could talk to or network with' I've put a couple of options on the table for people to consider, which makes it easier for them to answer the question. Note too that the question is always phrased in the third person – do you know someone who – and never as a closed direct question, such as the dreadful 'do you have a job for me?'

YOUR NETWORKING QUESTION

Think about what it is you want from people.
Look again at the examples given above, then write down here the question that best fits your needs and goals:

_____

_____

_____

PERSEVERANCE PAYS

Career change is always possible. Even in tough economic times, there are opportunities to make a change and head in a different direction. However, what all those who successfully changed their careers have in common is that they persevered – they all made sure their career engine had the power and resilience to get through the transition phase and into their new role. If we say that we want to make a career change, but know in our heart that we're not really sure about it, then don't do it. If we make a half-hearted start we run the risk of getting a half-hearted outcome. This could mean a nightmare scenario for us – we have left a job that paid the bills and are now struggling to find a new job, while needing to spend money to support our job hunting activities.

I worked with a business administrator who had had enough of his role and wanted to retrain as an accounts clerk. When I met him, his most unnerving comment to me was that he wanted to leave his current role in order to *force* himself to change jobs and get what he wanted, while openly admitting that he didn't have enough savings to support himself in the meantime. After our conversation and a review of the financial facts, he decided to stay put in his current role and save up to pay for the move.

Even though we may hate our current role, we still need to be realistic about the timescales ahead of us and plan sensibly, because it could take us 12 to 18 months to land the new job that we seek. Do you have the perseverance to last that long in transition?

BUDGET FOR RETRAINING

If we don't budget for our career change, we could cause our family hardship as we suddenly redirect housekeeping funds towards the skills we need to get a new job.

One of the best ways to facilitate a change is to invest in new skills, whether by completing a vocational course, post-graduate study or further professional exams. These tend to be expensive, relative to our disposable income, and we may need to increase our mortgage, take out a bank loan or ask our family for support. If we're in a large organisation, there may be funds available to enable us to retrain and make an internal move, so it's always worth finding out if we can raise some kind of corporate sponsorship.

When thinking about money, we need to check our assumptions and be prudent, so:

- How much money do you have set aside to fund your career change?
- Have you included a 20% top-up as a contingency fund, on the basis that there are always hidden costs and that life has a habit of turning out to be more expensive than we'd originally budgeted for?

ESSENTIAL RESOURCES

While we are reviewing our financial requirements, we can also take stock of the additional resources needed to move us in a new direction. When I started my business I had, quite literally, one biro, a book about coaching and access to my wife's computer. I didn't have a car because my company car had been returned, and so my first task was to make them an offer for it. I didn't have a huge amount of savings either, which although made life a bit scary for a while, helped me to be focussed and made me work much harder to get things up and running. Here's a checklist of resources you might need. What do you notice?

CAREER CHANGE RESOURCES

What do you not have enough of?
How can you counter the deficit?

Cash for retraining.
Time to attend training courses.
Space at home to study.
Three different, well-informed mentors.
The long-term support of your family.
A clear sense of your abilities and skill gaps.
Current contacts from within your new industry.
The humility to ask relevant questions and listen to the answers.
An action plan with milestones and deadlines.
A cash-flow forecast to see how your household finances will
be affected over the next two years.

An action plan is always useful, particularly when we want the support of our family. I coined the term *Bank of Family* a few years ago when talking to clients about the level of support they could rely on. To change our career, we need to withdraw goodwill from our Bank of Family in order to provide emotional capital for our career change. However, if we keep withdrawing and fail to repay the loan, it is likely that our family will run out of goodwill and will force us to change our plans. It could get messy.

Likewise, a cash-flow forecast is an essential item on our checklist because it predicts the future for us. If we have a household budget to manage, it's unwise to close our eyes to the possibility that this could suffer. Instead, we must be proactive and plan our income and expenditure so that we can fund our career change in an orderly fashion.

SAMPLE CASH-FLOW FORECAST

If you're not used to producing a cash-flow forecast, you can use the example below to build a more accurate picture of your financial situation. What the forecast seeks to do is track income and expenditure and provide a view of whether our bank balance goes up or down over time.

Month	Jan	Feb	Mar	Apr	May	Jun
Opening Balance	500	400	-300	-1,000	-1,300	-1,100
Income	+ 1,000	0	0	+ 500	+ 1,000	+ 1,000
Less Expenses						
Rent	300	300	300	300	300	300
Food	300	200	200	200	200	200
Travel	200	100	100	200	200	200
Bills	100	100	100	100	100	100
Leisure	200	0	0	0	0	0
Balance	400	-300	-1,000	-1,300	-1,100	-900

In the model above, you'll notice that our career change person leaves their job at the end of January and starts their new role in April. Because they get paid a month in arrears (their first pay packet isn't until May), they need to take £500 out of their savings in April to help reduce their overdraft. Notice too that their leisure budget is cut and their travel budget changes with their employment situation. A prudent approach makes good sense as it will take them a while to bring their bank account back into the black.

We could use a credit card to fund the gap, but be wary of the interest charges we're racking up – if we owe £10,000 then we may pay £3,000 *a year* in interest to service the debt, making credit cards an expensive choice. Better options to fund the change may include down-sizing our car, selling unwanted possessions at a car boot sale, raising a bank loan, extending our mortgage or dipping into savings.

If this cash-flow forecast was for your household finances, what would you do differently to fund the transition? In which month does your model go back into the black? Remember that it can take between six and twelve months to find a new job (if we're out of work), and a career change could add another six months to that.

CASE STUDY – GRAHAM

Graham was an engineer who ran a small business making metal components for exhaust systems, but he was bored. Every day was the same for him, and although he was 'the boss' he had the same people with the same problems and the same customers with the same demands, day in and day out. He decided to make a change and as such, sold the business to his senior manager, went back to university and completed a master's programme in Lean process improvement techniques. This included a two-day project in his local hospital, which was way out of his comfort zone in terms of culture and complexity, but he found that he thrived in the environment. The two days were challenging, busy and rewarding, and at the end of them he had identified a simple change that would enable patients to be seen more quickly by their consultant.

On completing his course, Graham applied for a variety of jobs and although he received offers from several factories, he was keen to work in the National Health Service (NHS). To make this happen, he contacted the hospital where he had completed his project and also asked all his course tutors if they knew of anyone relevant he could talk to. A tutor put him in contact with a senior change manager in the NHS – in networking terms, this is called a 'warm referral' because we ask someone to make the introduction for us, instead of having to write to them out of the blue.

Graham followed up with the contact, visited them and after much discussion, was offered a short-term contract as a change agent, which was soon extended. Although he didn't really have enough experience of working in a hospital environment, he had relevant professional knowledge and had built up a good rapport with the senior manager, who liked his enthusiasm.

Graham spent two years working successfully to deliver process improvements and then switched to running his own department after being promoted to a senior position. He is now a very happy Graham and the business he left behind seems to be a world away from the career that he now has.

SO WHAT?

A career change might be difficult. It might cost us a large amount of cash. It might put pressure on our families and create tension at home. It might take time to resolves details, learn new skills and acquire practical experience. It might be all of these things and more, and yet changing our career is an option open to all of us.

In today's modern workplace, career changes are a common occurence and they have allowed certain industries to recruit talented people. A good example of this is the teaching profession, which actively recruits from the commercial and service sectors, and each year draws in highly-qualified and motivated people who wish to swap growing profits for growing children. Having a background as a corporate manager, for example, can be a benefit to a school that need leaders to organise staff and take on responsibility.

With regards to career change, the things that matter the most are what we want to do with our lives and how much effort and discomfort we're prepared to put up with to achieve it. We can be ambitious, we can engage our physis to release the energy to make a change and we can network and create a pathway for ourselves. In addition, we don't have to know exactly which direction to fly our rocket in on day one – we can make a start and join the dots as we go.

LEARNING EXERCISE

We can change our career, if we really want to. We can use our skill and intuition to guide us and we can fly our rocket cautiously so that the ride is smooth and the direction easy to adjust. What counts is to make a start, so having read this chapter, what is one thing you will do to begin the next exciting phase of your modern career? Pause, think and note down here one easy little step you can take:

_____

_____

_____

9
Career Accelerators
– Flying Higher, Flying Faster –

COCKPIT QUESTION:
How visible and credible are you to the senior managers?

SETTING US UP FOR SUCCESS

If we don't learn from the past, we are doomed to fly our rocket round in a slow circle. Gaining a promotion is often not an accident and we can incorporate success into our career so that we are well thought of, get offered new projects and exciting roles. Success will help us to avoid the cut when times get tough and 10% of the workforce has to be politely asked to leave.

WHAT DO WE DO?

For each section in this chapter, we can ask ourselves 'do I do this already?' If we answer a hearty 'yes' in each case then all is well and good, but if not, the invitation is there for us to really think about it – what will we *choose* from this chapter to help us accelerate our career and fly faster or fly higher?

SECTION 1: PEOPLE SKILLS

We've already seen how essential people skills are a key ingredient of our *Organisational Impact Score* and here we will look at them in more detail. People skills include how we interact with our colleagues and our line managers and what they really think of us – whether they like us, trust us and want to have us on their team.

1.1 EASY TO DO BUSINESS WITH

Are you easy to do business with? When a line manager asks us to do a new task do we smile and accept in a friendly way or do we scowl and grumble and huff and puff? I used to huff and puff and grumble that I was too busy to do the work, and it never occurred to me that my boss might have been quite busy too and was simply trying to delegate the workload. I was naïve for sure and it also never occurred to me that I was storing up resentment – eventually he decided I was too much of a nuisance and waved goodbye to me.

1.2 ENGAGING WITH PEOPLE

When we engage with people, we show interest, take note of what they're saying and enjoy their company. We become the kind of person that people like to have in the organisation and are considered to be someone who brings harmony to the workplace. This doesn't mean that we have to be a natural 'people person' – we can still be engaging and at the same time like to work quietly on our own in a corner. The difference is about how we react when people engage with us – do we pay attention to them or do we shrug and shoo them away with a dismissive wave of our hand?

1.3 BEING PRESENT

When we're at work are we really there in mind and body? Or do we park our body at a work station and let our brain drift away and daydream about what we're having for dinner, where we're going on holiday and what's worth watching on television that night? When we go to a meeting do we sit attentively, alert to the people around us and what they are saying, or do we stifle a yawn and draw little stars on our notepad? Many of us have smartphones and the temptation to check our Facebook feeds and our Twitter accounts might be too much to ignore. We fool ourselves that we're only checking our phones intermittently, without realising that our line manager is watching us from the corner of the office and getting increasingly fed up. When we go to work we need to be in the building and alert to our surroundings – people notice when we are present and they like us for it. They also resent us when we ignore what they're saying, check our phones or draw little boxes in the corner of our briefing paper.

1.4 BEING VISIBLE

While being present means being alert to our immediate surroundings, being visible means coming to the attention of the senior management. When there is a redundancy situation and people have to make choices about who stays and who goes, there is always a grey area of doubt and if the senior managers don't know who we are, they are more likely to get rid of us than if they know us and like us. We can enhance our career by being more visible to the decision-makers, so when a new opportunity arises we will tend to feature more prominently in their thinking. Three good ways to enhance our career by becoming visible are:

1. **Apply for internal roles.** If we get them, that's great. If we don't, we become someone who looks ambitious and we get talked about by the senior managers.

2. **Join committees.** If there is a cross-functional committee, such as a Christmas Party organising team, join it and take part – these are often sponsored by a senior manager and they will be able to see us performing well and contributing to the wider success of the organisation.

3. **Ask for a senior mentor.** Many senior managers are happy to help develop talent within their organisation and spending one-to-one time with a director each month is a great way to get to know them. Familiarity breeds respect and they will get to see us learning and growing, and as such, will be more inclined to help us develop our career when an opportunity arises.

1.5 BUILDING THE PSYCHOLOGICAL

When we communicate with another person, we operate on two levels. The first is the surface level – the words we're saying and the look on our face – and the second is the sub-surface level.

This is known as the psychological level and it's about what we're *really* saying to the other person.[12] There will be times when we're doing our best to be polite and yet our body language and our tone of voice tell a different story – we could be *saying* 'thank you' and might actually be *sending* them a 'go away' message. In order to develop our career and strengthen our future options, we need to 'build the psychological level' with people so that our surface words are matched with sub-surface feelings.

Because we can't see other people's feelings, we can't build this rapport directly – it is the result of our interaction with them and the information they collect about us from other people. Are we considered to be honest, trustworthy, consistent, and genuinely friendly, have useful ideas and are someone to be relied upon? Or are we deceitful, mean spirited and vengeful?

We need to establish our reputation as a person who embodies useful work traits and who is trustworthy and reliable. That way people feel good about us on a psychological level, trust us and will want to work with us. What can you do to establish a good reputation?

- Deliver work on time?
- Keep a confidence?
- Be genuinely polite?
- Smile when you shake hands?
- Take time to get to know people?
- Be seen as fair minded?
- Have ambition that doesn't seek to trample people unfairly?

[12] Eric Berne (1966) wrote about the 'psychological level' that affects the agreements we have with other people. On the surface we may agree to complete a task by a given point in time, but underneath, where we all have secret feelings and hidden thoughts, if we don't like the person and don't trust them it's likely that we won't do the work and will find an excuse to avoid it, despite having apparently agreed to do it.

1.6 MEDAL DAYS

All athletes train hard for key competitions, but we don't tend to see this – we only notice them when they win a medal and are cheered by fans and given glowing reports in the press. As a medal winner, they become a 'somebody' who might earn a sponsorship deal, be invited to participate in more important events and generally advance their career to the next level. It's the same for us and in order to accelerate our career we need to notice opportunities for us to earn 'organisational medals'.

Pause for a moment and think about the next few weeks in your place of work. Which days could be 'medal days'? Perhaps when you have to organise a site visit for a visiting director, deliver a presentation to a key customer, attend an important meeting, or deliver the results of a key project? All of these are opportunities to shine and to be recognised for our good work. Have you ever been an 'employee of the month'? This is a great way to get noticed by winning a medal.

GOLD MEDAL CASE STUDY – MEGHAN

I once coached a lecturer called Meghan, who had just started a new job and wanted to make a good impression. I asked her what she needed to do to become an employee of the month. Not knowing the answer, Meghan chatted with a couple of senior managers, who said it was for outstanding work. Armed with this information, she then spent time reorganising her course so that she could apply for state funding and generate more income for her organisation.

When she'd completed this work in record time, she told her line manager, who smiled and remembered the conversation about employee of the month – and two weeks later she was awarded that accolade. In fact, she went on to win it twice within six months and when I last spoke to her she was loving her new job, because her bosses valued what she did and had given her more responsibility and now involved her in strategic decision making.

GOLD MEDAL CASE STUDY – ADRIAN

A week before their company's vice president was due to visit the factory, Adrian's operations director held a meeting with his line managers to outline what he needed from each of them – namely a five-minute presentation about their department to show how well they were doing. Adrian was the most junior manager in the room and was often pushed about by the others because he ran a tiny section of the factory, and dealt with a new product that few people understood and even fewer had any time for. However, he was a proactive powerhouse who had transformed his corner from an untidy jumble of desks and boxes into a super-efficient production cell. He was also full of energy and ideas and this made him a natural presenter.

The vice president visited and sat politely though the other presentations, which all lacked sparkle and gently patronised him as an ignorant senior manager who was too remote to really understand their departments. Adrian was different – he told a clear story and showed pictures to explain the 'before and after' layouts and how he had reduced build time and increased quality so that they had a 10-fold increase in output at no extra cost. He delivered his presentation with real passion for his work and spoke sincerely and articulately for five minutes and then spent another 30 minutes chatting with the vice president and answering his questions. It was a great medal-winning day for him and as a direct result, his director promoted him to manage a new production unit and the vice president added him to an international improvement team.

The other managers had all missed the opportunity to win a medal. What would you have done if you had been one of the managers asked to present that day?

SECTION 2: TECHNICAL SKILLS

Technical skills are the performance-related areas that determine how well we do our job and add value to our host organisation. They combine trainable skills and innate talents that we are born with.

2.1 GENERATING GOOD NEWS

This comes at the top of the list because as we've discussed earlier, it's no good working hard only to be ignored or to have someone else claim the credit for our efforts. It's okay to tell people what we have done well and to give our line manager good news and to make sure that they're aware of our part in it. This is what good public relations is all about. In my experience, the best way to do this is to send our line manager a two-line email highlighting something that went particularly well. Consider these questions:

- When did you last send your manager an email to share one of your successes?
- When did you go out of your way to buy your boss a coffee to say thanks for his support?
- When will you find time to share three pieces of good news with your line manager this month?

Our line manager is likely to be divorced from the daily details of our work and will relish positive feedback and good news. It gives him something to pass up the chain to his boss, which in turn creates a positive ripple of public relations up into the ranks of senior management.

2.2 BEING BRILLIANT

Modesty can sometimes help us if we're surrounded by arrogant types and want to be quietly competent and take a 'less is more approach'. We need to be careful though, because given the busy nature of people at work, a 'less is more' approach can, in reality, go unnoticed. We want to be brilliant at something so that we have a core skill the organisation values. We all have a strength that shines above the others and it might take a few years to work out what it is. For example, I'm great at presentations and yet it took an inspired teacher to unlock my potential – thereafter I was always asked by the managing director to present to customers and it was a great way to create positive public relations and be well thought of.

If we play to our strengths we will excel, use less effort and will create good feedback for ourselves. Although this makes perfect sense, how many people do you know who are currently struggling in a job where they can't shine? Where are you now? Are you playing to your latent strengths, or in denial and, for example, working hard to be a bank administrator when you're a natural artist?

- What do you consider to be your best work-related strength?
- What do your colleagues often praise you for?
- In your last appraisal, what did you get the best feedback for?
- How can you spend more time using your key strength?

BEING BRILLIANT CASE STUDY – RALPH

In the first part of his modern career, Ralph had graduated with a history degree and little sense of what he wanted to do for work, and had ended up as a trainee manager in an insurance business. This involved typing numbers into the company software, running product development projects and attempting to motivate his little team of clerks to really love the paper chase in the office and enjoy filling forms.

It was a good steady job, paid well and he could drink as much free coffee as he could cope with. The big problem for Ralph was that his manager was only interested in what he did and not what he thought. All the praise he received was for doing things, and if he was 'caught thinking' he was invariably scolded with a pout and a comment that 'he clearly didn't have enough work to do that day'.

The organisation sent him away on a leadership course that involved lots of thinking time. Ralph loved it and excelled in it – so much so that on his return he asked to change roles from a line manager to an internal development manager, responsible for setting up training courses and mentoring new staff. The transfer was a great success, for the simple reason that Ralph was far better at thinking than he was at repetitive transactions. As a result he quickly excelled and turned into a much happier and more settled employee.

2.3 NETWORKING

If we want to accelerate our career, we need to invest time in networking around the organisation. We can do this by getting to know:

- *People on our floor* – introduce ourselves when we meet others at the coffee machine.
- *People on other floors* – ask to spend time shadowing other departments to improve company knowledge.

- *People at the head office* – offer our services to inter-departmental teams and projects.

It's quite common for people to wince when I tell them that networking is key to career success, and that's okay – there are plenty of things that we didn't like at first, but which we have grown used to or learnt to tolerate. It's all about the goals we have; if they are something we really want then the journey becomes less onerous and we will work harder to achieve them. If the thought of networking seems too gruesome to you and you know in your heart that although you understand the need for it, you're not going to do it, I would reflect on the following questions:

- Are your goals really what you want?
- What would your goals have to be in order for you to embrace networking and use it to accelerate your career?

2.4 EDUCATION

If we wish to enhance our career and take on a bigger role, we need the skills to do so. We also need to be proactive in gaining them and not wait for the organisation to provide for us. Increasingly, as people build portfolio careers from several smaller roles, or move between roles with greater frequency, there isn't time to invest in them. Given that many organisations now ask people to source and bring their own computing device to work; they also will begin to expect people to be proactive and sort out their own training needs. While they may be prepared to bear some of the cost of this, we may sometimes have to pay for it entirely. What matters is that we get the training we need to propel our career upwards, instead of moaning that we're never sent on any useful training courses.

I speak from experience here and, as previously mentioned, have invested over £20,000 of my own money in my development over the last 10 years. At first, I kept thinking that 'this would be the last year' and that I could divert the spend into more wages for me, until I finally realised that if I didn't develop myself I wouldn't be able to create new products, win new customers and remain in business. My training and development budget was an integral part of my own business success, and without it, my career rocket would have begun to cough and splutter and lose height.

Many human resources departments now lack the time to organise bespoke training for individual members of staff, but are happy to help motivated people who do the research for them and present them with an application form to sign. Think about these questions:

- How much do you spend on your own development?
- When did you last research a training course and make it easy for your line manger to say yes to you attending it?

Making it easy for people to say yes is often the key to success. This can mean us offering to pay for part of the course, or offering to complete it in our own time, or in a way that reduces the impact on our work. For example, I now use Skype to teach people coaching skills at their desks, which removes all travel time and makes it easier for their line manager to agree to.

Before you read on, ask yourself:

- What can you do to help yourself get the training you need to accelerate your career?

2.5 ADDING VALUE & REMOVING WASTE

If we just do our job each day and go home, we'll have fulfilled the basic contract we have with our employer, but we won't have shone as brightly as we could have and we're less likely to be promoted. In the days of the traditional career ladder, we could count the years to our next promotion and all we needed to do was turn up to work and the reward was ours. In the climate of the *modern career* – where it's up to us to ride our rocket and be proactive – it's becoming essential to be seen as someone who improves processes, removes waste from the system, can be relied upon to save money and actively welcomes change. Adding value and being responsive to change is a must-have technical skill and gets us noticed as somebody who is worth keeping.

To improve a process, we need to do two things;

- Measure the process so we can clearly see where the delays are located.
- Map the process so we can reveal its inner complexity.

We don't need to use a complex methodology to do this and instead can easily write down each stage in a list and add processing times to them. We then need to work out which bits of the process add value, which is often a frighteningly small amount. Here are some examples:

- When ink is printed onto paper to create a book, we add value.
- When a doctor sees a patient, that adds value.
- When a client signs a form, that adds value.
- When wheels are added to a car to make it drivable, that adds value.

Everything else is a waste, because although it might feel productive, it doesn't add any value. Storing paper, waiting to see the doctor, making a mistake on a form and leaving a car up on a hoist adds no value and wastes resources.

There are eight different types of waste to look out for and they are:[13]

1. **Overproduction** – where we waste resources by making too much.
2. **Waiting** – an hour lost waiting can never be regained.
3. **Transporting** – moving things around adds no value (think about food miles).
4. **Inappropriate processing** – making a task unnecessarily complex, perhaps by printing 10 pages of reports when a one-page summary of key exceptions would suffice.
5. **Unnecessary inventory** – turning cash into stock; when we buy too much it takes up space and is likely to get lost, stolen or damaged.
6. **Unnecessary movement** – think about the ergonomics of

[13] Reference *The Quality 60*, John Bicheno (1988).

our working environment; do we have to keep twisting to reach for the diary, is the printer within reach, do we have to keep borrowing a stapler from the desk behind us?

7. **Defects** – if we make a bad product, it contains all the other wastes and we have to start again. This is why so many organisations find ways to improve the quality of their products and services because it removes waste and improves output.

8. **People** – we can under-utilise people by asking them to perform tasks which add no value or are way below their skill set.

CAREER TOP TIP

How to remove waste:
1. **Stand still.** Observe people at work. Who is actually doing something productive and who is killing time?
2. **Look for piles of paper work.** These tell us when people are working hard and are under-resourced, or when they are lacking clear performance targets, or have got themselves into a muddle and need an attentive colleague to help them out.
3. **Walk the process.** This is a great way to make the invisible come to life. For example, if we follow the route of a product or a patient, we will soon see where there is waste.
4. **Mine our frustrations.** We often know what is causing us to waste time and effort, and if we stop and write down exactly what is frustrating us, we will see where the waste is.

Good employees do their job to a reasonable standard. *Great* employees do the job and find ways to improve it so that their host organisation benefits. Then when we make improvements we need to measure them because numbers are objective, tell the story for us and are easier to remember. When we think about accelerating our career, we can ask:

- Where can we save time?
- How can we add more value?
- What can we do to save money?

SO WHAT?

We can set ourselves up for success and can make it easier for our career to accelerate into higher reaches of management, or into new and more exciting roles. If we develop a good instinct for our PR, maintain a warm disposition towards our colleagues, play to our strengths, embrace change and improve the organisation, we will be well placed to fly higher and faster. Being a lonely and remote iconoclast isn't going to help us. Nor are we expected to be someone that we're not, or turn into the life and soul of the office, or make the coffee all the time – what matters here is a consistent and positive approach to our work, because that helps others build trust in us.

We can know that certain traits, attitudes and skills will help us to accelerate our career and it's up to us to decide which ones we want to use and how often to use them.

LEARNING EXERCISE

We want to make life simple for ourselves and the trick is to do things that feel natural and which we are drawn towards, rather than forcing ourselves into an unnatural shape. Skip back through this chapter and choose one item from each section to do more of and write them down here:

Section 1 – People Skills
I will be doing more of this in the future:

_____

_____

Section 2 – Technical Skills
I will be doing more of this in the future:

_____

_____

10
The Career Killers
– Becoming Toxic –

COCKPIT QUESTION:
How familiar are you with the impact of your
stress-related behaviour?

PRESSURE OVERLOAD

We discussed the topic of awareness earlier and how important it is to successful career management. What we also have to account for are any deep-seated behaviours that might derail our progress. The more pressure we are under, the more these traits are likely to show and their effects can be catastrophic, because they have the power to create a sustained bad impression or can deal one fatal blow to our reputation. If we become toxic, our career is probably over and we need to change course promptly.

LABELS STICK

We are all able to learn and we all learn in different ways and at different speeds, which is fine if we're balanced and reasonable.

However, we can somtimes have a tendency to be unthinking, have bubbling emotions that cause us to lead a conversation with our mouth and not with our brain, or are simply unaware of our child-like behaviour that leaves us open to accusations of immaturity. This can happen when we blurt out something and reveal the grumpy child sulking beneath our carefully polished exterior, when we complain bitterly about being treated unfairly, to the point that people lose sympathy for us, or if our reaction to a reasonable request is well outside of reasonable practices and accepted behavioural norms.

People remember outbursts longer than they remember all the positive days, and when we lose control we hand others a golden opportunity to cut us down to size with a withering comment or to dismiss our strengths by labelling us as immature. Sadly, labels have a habit of sticking as people only need one piece of evidence to keep it in place. For example, we might be a reliable employee and have worked diligently for a year, and then have a row with a colleague who has been needling us, allowing our detractors to label us as 'stroppy'. We may carry on working happily, but if we have a row with that employee again we leave ourselves open to being thought of as a 'difficult character' when, in fact, our actions were the result of extreme provocation.

THE CAREER KILLERS MODEL

To help understand how we might be labelled by others, we can think of four classic workplace dimensions and how, when under pressure, our behaviour moves out of a reasonable 'sweet spot' to become more extreme, causing distress to those around us and perhaps even stalling our rocket in mid-flight.

THE CAREER KILLERS MODEL

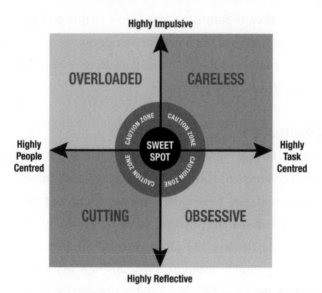

This is a model of how our behaviour distorts under pressure. To identify which category we are most likely to fall into, we can think about the two axes and put a cross on them to show how far along each one we tend to go. We can then find out which quadrant that tends to put us in by projecting out from each axis to where the lines would cross. For example, if we marked a point half way along the *task centric* axis and the *reflective axis*, that would put us firmly in the middle of the *Obsessive* quadrant. The further away from the middle we are, out towards the bottom right hand corner, the more pronounced our obsessive behaviour is likely to be.

Here is the model explained in more detail:

SWEET SPOT

If we are here then we are mature and grounded and can cope well with pressure and the demands of a challenging role. If we can use our skills and maintain our awareness, we can remain in this sweet spot and will enjoy taking on more responsibility and earning well-deserved promotions.

CAUTION ZONE

As we get pushed up against a deadline, a difficult task or the prospect of completing a stretching challenge, we will move away from the sweet spot. This is when we need to stop and think about what we are doing and what we could do to take better care of ourselves. We can take a break, get help, do something different, or we can continue grinding away and moving further from reasonable justifiable behaviour and out towards an extreme.

PEOPLE CENTRIC VS. TASK CENTRIC

When we're under pressure, we may find ourselves drawn to people and keen to make sure we have company. If we're people focussed then we tend to want to be in the company of people and notice what they say and how they behave towards us. Our senses are more alert to other people's moods and their needs and wants. Our own needs begin to take second place to those of people around us. A classic indicator of being people focussed is, when we have a task to complete, we telephone a friend, walk to the coffee machine to find someone to talk to, or check our email and have electronic conversations. We need people around us, either in real life or as social media avatars.

If we're task focussed, we like to withdraw and work in our own space, perhaps by moving to a quiet office away from the noise, or by plugging in our music player and headphones to isolate us from the world. Task-focussed people tend to be less appreciative of the needs of others and, in extremes, may be thought of as cold, uncaring or selfish. That doesn't mean that we are such – these are just labels that other people may attach to us.

- Which side do you tend to slide into when under pressure – people or task?

IMPULSIVE VS. REFLECTIVE

This axis is designed to encourage us to think about how we respond to new things, because as organisations change and develop they tend to value people who sensibly embrace new ways of working and sideline those who make the adoption of new policies hard work.

If we are impulsive, we like to embrace new problems and opportunities and welcome the distraction they bring to our routines. Developing organisations can be an uphill struggle for many line managers and they like impulsive types because their willing acceptance makes life a little easier for them. However, if we are too impulsive then we make snap decisions, act in haste, are poor managers of risk and can't really be relied upon to 'do the right thing' because our behaviour is spontaneous and changes with each new stimulus. We become a firework perpetually going off, as we jump at each new idea and sweep our desk clean to begin a new and exciting task, without thinking about the work we already have piled up.

If we are reflective, we like to take time to think. We like to ponder a new idea and think about its merits and its pitfalls, or what our part in its success could be and what questions we have. This is a more cautious approach and it makes us a better manager of risk and more reliable when dealing with difficult situations. The impulsive person may hit on the right answer, but may have taken several attempts to get there, whereas the reflective person takes their time, weighs up options and eventually comes to a good answer. However, when they are rushed for time or face a complex situation, reflective people often become over-burdened with questions to ask and possibilities to explore and constantly seek new information, afraid of making a mistake and wanting to be sure that they 'have a complete picture' before making a move.

While the overly impulsive person may be labelled as being speedy, reckless or risk-taking, the overly reflective person may be labelled slow, overly cautious or risk averse.

- Which end do you tend to gravitate towards when under pressure – impulsive or reflective?

PEOPLE CENTRIC & IMPULSIVE = OVERLOADED

If we're people centric, we will tend to notice others and the work they do and the stress they are labouring under. This 'noticing' of other people combines with our tendency for impulsive, generous behaviour and we will often stop what we're doing to make them a cup of tea, tidy their papers or perhaps even offer to do their work. They often won't even have to ask for support because they're used to our energetic helpfulness, and we're soon *overloaded* and over capacity as we move work from their desk to ours.

Our dilemma – is that we have our own work to do, but we don't want to let others down. The dilemma is resolved by us accepting the work from them because we can always work a bit later into the evening to complete our own tasks.

The con – the con (the bit of twisted logic that we use to fool ourselves) here is that we don't want to let these people down, because if we do they might not like us anymore. If it's our line manager who is in need of help or who asks us to help them, we really don't want to let them down, because they might think less of us. As a result, we become overloaded and our own work starts to be neglected – which means we've let them down. It's a con because they won't think less of us if we do our own work and politely encourage them to find other people to help them.

The career-killing outcome – even though we think we're being helpful, we might be labelled as someone who is *poor at time management*. People can be ruthless in asking for our help or accepting our kind offer, and then criticise us when we don't have time to do our own work. If we have no time, we can't be trusted to handle more prestigious tasks.

The antidote to being overloaded – is to keep our to-do list in clear sight so we can see our capacity limitations. We also need to be clear about the consequences of taking on more work, so that our manager knows where to shift priorities and agree on what tasks we can delay. We can learn to say 'yes, *and* I can do the work tomorrow', or 'yes, I can do a part of it next week' instead of 'yes, I'll do the work now'.[14] We can also know that friendship isn't just based on how helpful we are – we can let people do their work and we can help them out as appropriate, but we can't buy friendship by doing their job for them.

PEOPLE CENTRIC & REFLECTIVE = CUTTING

If we're people centric and reflective, we will hear what others say and how they say it and will notice when they are kind to us and also when they're less than honest, or if they ignore us. Because we like to think and then think some more, we start to wonder what is behind their behaviour towards us. People often ignore the positives and focus on the negatives, and we begin to think that they're out to get us. We are *cutting* towards them in conversation, as our voice is edged with reservation and distrust. We might start to gossip against them, or be openly dismissive when asked reasonably to undertake a task.

Our dilemma – we want to believe that we haven't done anything wrong, but now that we've noticed a supposed change in their behaviour, we keep finding more evidence that they have a problem with us. The dilemma is resolved by talking to friends and sharing our concerns, but when they try to sooth us we don't really believe them because we know best.

The con – is that we think do know best, when in fact we

---

[14] Saying 'yes, and…' is much easy than saying 'no' because it allows us to put other people's requirements in context with our own.

are playing out our own insecurities. These are based on how other people might have treated us in the past, and in order to protect ourselves, we see patterns of negative behaviour towards us where none exist.

The career-killing outcome – is that we become labelled as *difficult*, and we are convinced that the other person (or people) is plotting against us, doesn't like us or is scheming to remove us. We begin to bore people with our theories and polarise opinion in the office. Inevitably, one of them tells the perpetrator that 'Richard really has it in for you' and then *we* become the problem. We have allowed a self-fulfilling prophecy to come to life. People don't want to work with us and our line manger re-assigns us or we face redundancy, which of course is what we knew they were plotting all along!

The antidote to being cutting – is to remind ourselves of all the *objective evidence* and to include the good and the bad in our thinking, instead of just the bad. People are busy, forgetful and have their own worlds to manage and often have no idea that they appear to be ignoring us. Everyone has a life and story and we can't presume to know theirs. If we are genuinely struggling, we need to take our fears outside of work so we can talk through things with a neutral coach or mentor and get their more objective and dispassionate views on our thinking. We can also have a conversation with the person we have a problem with by being assertive, in a polite way, and saying 'when you say [insert their words], I feel [insert your feeling] and I'd like to talk about it as I may be getting the wrong impression.'

TASK CENTRIC & REFLECTIVE = OBSESSIVE

If we're task focussed, we keep our heads down and concentrate on completing the work in front of us. We tend to ignore people or push them away, as our concentration narrows our gaze and we only see the project we're currently working on. If we're reflective, we think carefully about what we're doing and will want to do a great job, get the details right and avoid mistakes. As the pressure builds and because we want to do a brilliant job we over-think the options, add more detail than is required and over-complicate the task. We become *obsessive* and lose sight of the required standard, assuming that more is better.

Our dilemma – we want to do a great job and be well thought of, although we know that there are other tasks building up behind us. We struggle to reconcile the need to do this task well with the need to simply finish it and go on to the next task. In the end, we stick with our 'more is better' approach and let the other tasks suffer.

The con – for obsessives is that if they put in less effort they think they will be thought less of, or will be criticised for a tiny mistake or a missing detail. Of course, the truth is that it's all about meeting the required standard and not our fantasy high standards.

The career-killing outcome – is that we become labelled as a *perfectionist*, with its overtones of inappropriate detail, time wasting and inflexibility, because we stick rigidly to our task until we have finished it. We might also be labelled as a fussy or indecisive person as we dither and search for *just one more* fact before finally making our decision. Although we may do a great job, we only do *one* job and this narrow focus means that people can't see how we can handle a bigger job if we're steadily 'plodding' through the one we currently have.

The antidote to being obsessive – is to agree on the required standard at the start of the piece of work and to have clearly defined review points, so we can pause and get feedback without getting carried away by small details. We can know when enough is enough and give ourselves a break from adding in more layers of detail. We can also make a choice to do a good enough job, instead of doing an over-blown job and killing our career.

TASK CENTRIC & IMPULSIVE = CARELESS

If we're task focussed and we like new things, we will tend to volunteer for new assignments and collect new tasks to do. This affects our capacity to actually do the work, as well as increases the chances that the output will be slapdash. Unlike the obsessive character who works away slavishly at one task, we happily begin projects and initially make a great impression with our enthusiasm and our willingness to say 'yes I'll do that' to anything on offer. Unlike the overloaded person who is too busy doing other people's work to do their own, the careless person creates a fountain of new work for themselves and sets up high expectations from their line manager. If we're a careless person we're often described as 'an impressive new hire' until the line manager wants projects to be completed and realises that we're too busy starting new tasks to finish the work we already have.

Our dilemma – we want to excel at work and yet we don't

want to be bored, so we decide to excel by doing lots of things to impress our line manager. We are acting out of awareness and enjoying the excitement of starting new projects without thinking about how we will complete them all.

The con – for careless types is that they worry they will be caught looking idle if they don't have enough work to do. Instead, they over compensate and create too much work, which sets up a timebomb of incomplete work and missed deadlines.

The career-killing outcome – is that we become labelled as someone who *doesn't deliver* on time and to the right standard. Delivering half a project report three days late isn't going to impress people and because we have over promised and under delivered, we have made our line manager look foolish. He was impressed with our early energy and happily told his manager about all the great things they could expect to see from us, but now has to explain why we failed to deliver and why he didn't keep a closer eye on us.

The antidote to carelessness – is to plan our work load so we can work out what our capacity is and when our deadlines are. This way, we can start no more than six projects and can run them concurrently and deliver outcomes on time. We can know that there is always more work to be done and that if we pass up on a few projects and focus on *delivering* the work we have, we will eventually have the capacity *and* the track record to choose bigger and more prestigious projects.

CASE STUDY – ALISON

People don't tend to kill their career in one single bound, although it can happen. Years ago I was rude about a senior manager to the whole office, not realising that as I had stood up to speak he had entered the room and was now standing silently behind me while I ranted. In my defence I was young and immature, but it was still inexcusable of me and deeply humiliating for him. He later tried to make my role redundant – even though I didn't report to him – and although I was saved, the shock of a close escape was a wake-up call.

Alison was different. She managed to ruin her career one late report at a time because of her *carelessness*. Alison was a talented analyst and with the commercial experience and insight that her not-for-profit organisation highly valued, she began her role on a high note. She started projects, was full of ideas and was a very credible manager, so of course she was quickly promoted to a senior position and given more freedom to operate.

The problem was that, in this new role, she was more exposed to working with other senior managers and had to provide them with feasibility studies and expert analysis. Her day-book was always bulging with paperwork and she rushed about starting projects and creating the impression of someone dynamic and purposeful.

However, when she had to present a strategy review paper to her board six months later, it all came crashing down. Having already become exasperated with her for submitting late and inconsistent work, her director had specifically sat down and walked her through his expectations for this paper. He noticed that during the meeting she didn't take notes and instead just nodded politely. The day before the board meeting, Alison handed in her strategy report to her incredulous director, who was aghast that it was a hand-written set of rough notes clipped to last year's report. Alison sealed her fate when she saw his reaction and casually commented,

'Oh yeah, I did some checking and there wasn't much to add since last year, so I thought I'd keep it the same and just add a few notes.'

Can you imagine preparing for an important meeting as a director and having a senior manager let you down like that? It was the final straw and a week later Alison was put on a performance review, which ended with her being overlooked for promotion and moved to a different part of the organisation. She had killed her career by being *careless*.

SO WHAT?

We tend to begin our career as immature and gullible youngsters, our eyes open to the world around us and our brains not always fully engaged as we struggle to acclimatise to our new working environment. For the first six months, all we can do is to fly our rocket very carefully and try to make as few mistakes as possible. When we're under stress we tend to default to tried and tested behaviours that have kept us safe at home, at school, at university, or in the sports team with our friends. Therefore, the quicker we find out which career-killing traits we have, the better we are able to ride our rocket successfully and continue our modern career in style.

LEARNING EXERCISE

When we first look at the Career Killers model it's tempting to skip over it and assume we sit on the sweet spot in the centre and have nothing to worry about. If this is the case, talk to a friend or a trusted colleague and ask them to assess you. Once you know which zone you tend to fall in when under pressure, write the answer below and include one thing that you can do differently, to make a positive difference in the future:

A) My tendency is to be overloaded / cutting / obsessive / careless. (Please circle one)

B) One thing I can do differently to avoid killing my career is to:

_____

_____

11
An Essential Guide
To Career Trends
– Preparing For The Future –

IS THIS REALLY AN *ESSENTIAL* GUIDE?

Yes. It will help us to embrace the future positively and will encourage us to keep our eyes open.

A TEAM OF EXPERTS

Given that the future is both tantalisingly close and unknowable in absolute terms, I recruited a crack squad of senior professionals, recruiters, social media experts and clear thinkers to contribute to this chapter. It's dangerous to speculate on our own as all we do is give voice to our assumptions and prejudices. However, by taking a group approach, we build a much more coherent and reliable picture and what follows here is a combination of all our thinking.

As you read the following sections think about if you agree, disagree or find yourself mentally tucking away thoughts for future reference. Discussion is valuable because it generates new thoughts, opportunities and resolutions to problems. Apathy is disastrous, so whatever you think when you read the rest of this chapter, at least you *are* thinking.

USEFUL GAZING INTO THE FUTURE

We can look into the future and feel anxious, or we can look again and make an informed assessment about what we perceive will happen. This chapter is intended to be useful, as well as thought provoking, so the emphasis is on practical predictions and commentary that reflects trends and changes which are:

- Already on the horizon.
- Moving from the innovators group to the early adopters group (3-D printing, for example).
- Moving from the early adopters group to the early majority (working at home, for example).[15]

DON'T BE AN OSTRICH

We have a choice to make – we can keep our head in the sand or we can look to the future and keep an eye on developing trends. The problem with not taking the latter course of action is that we can miss opportunities and leave ourselves vulnerable. I recently worked with a senior manager who wanted career coaching to make sure he was on top of his game at work and was able to keep delivering added value – he didn't want to wait 6 months for his next appraisal to find out how well he was doing. As part

---

[15] Reference: *Diffusion of Innovation*, Everett Rogers (1962). His classification of how innovations spread through a population group invites us to think which group we may be in and what the implications are for us when considering future trends. The groups and their % size of the population are – innovators (2.5%), early adopters (13.5%), early majority (34%), late majority (34%) and laggards (16%).

of this work we talked about social media and how he could use it to market his products. He winced and said:

'Oh Richard, I knew you'd talk about social media sooner or later. Do I really have to get in involved with all that *twittering* nonsense?'

What do you think my answer was?

NOBODY IS FUTURE-PROOF

It's tempting to argue that there are some careers which are immune to the vagaries of changing technological, sociological and geographical trends, but that's a myth. Ship building, mining and the decline of high street shops are all testaments to that. In today's modern career, we need to pay attention to technology, changing tastes and new ways of working.

If we run a tea room, our basic skills will probably not change much in the next 20 years, although we need to embrace new ideas because they are often responsible for ensuring that we remain in business. If we miss a trend, are out-competed by more technologically savvy competitors, or are unable to successfully recruit new talent, our business could be facing a slow decline. I've noticed that most of my local tea shops have Facebook fan pages, promote new menus on Twitter and engage with people so that they're more inclined to pop in and enjoy a scone. Consider these two questions:

- How future-proof is your current role?
- What warning signs do you need to act on?

GROUP P & GROUP M

The working world will become more sharply divided between people who have professional level skills (Group P) and those who have more menial skills (Group M). Previously, there was a sharper distinction between management and non-management, with managers often having generalist skills and the non-managers having craft and trade skills. The current trend is to value apprenticeships and hands-on experience and this means people who belong to Group P will have to make sure they have relevant practical application time to support academic qualifications.

People who are employed at a low level in high-speed processing environments such as call centres, fast food restaurants and warehouse stores will still travel to work and have similar conditions as they would today. There is nothing wrong in being in this group – society needs all sorts of occupations to be filled in order to function properly.

People who belong to Group P will increasingly need to become experts in their field so that they are hired for their knowledge or their specific craft skills. However, they will tend to work from home or from collaborative hubs and their customer base will extend across an entire country, or between other countries that speak similar languages.

The general role of the 'manager' will continue to decline. People from Group P will command higher salaries and fees by being recognised as leaders in their field. This also means that education will be a career-long requirement for these professional people in the way that it already is for doctors or accountants, for example.

Skills are important, and the more we are seen as an expert, the easier it will be for us to move around the job market and earn a living when economies dip. If you're in Group P:

- How much of an expert are you now?
- When did you last read an industry-relevant book or attend a conference?

NOMADS & SILOS

Given the requirement for organisations to be responsive to changing market forces and only hire skills when needed, there will tend to be a greater number of self-employed people and single-handed consultancies. In 2010, 15% of the population across Europe was self-employed[16]. This indicates that there is already a sizable population group who work outside of traditional employed life and this group will continue to grow in size as:

- Younger people are increasingly setting up their own businesses as a way to begin their careers.
- Public service sectors create waves of new consultancy businesses when they make cuts to staff and then hire them back on flexible contracts.
- Mid-life career changers try self-employment as an antidote to unpleasant, or restrictive, corporate experiences.

This population group is free of corporate restrictions, making them flexible and able to respond to new opportunities across a wide geographic area, riding trends and following the herd from one new project to the next. In the way that mercenaries were

---

[16] Reference: *European Employment Observatory Review*: 'Self-Employment in Europe' (2012).

hired in the middle ages, we will tend to see these 'freelance nomads' moving freely within the job market and increasing the trend towards globalisation.

In instances where organisations do need to house people in functional teams, there could be an increase in silo working, where departments act as individual fiefdoms and tend not to communicate with other departments because of the rise in specialisation. The use of social media will allay some of the worst effects of this, assuming we know who we can talk to. Overall, when thinking about flexibility:

- If you decided to become more of a nomadic worker, what would need to change?
- Who can support you in your travels?

TREND HOPPING

We currently think of people as moving between jobs, but we will increasingly move between skill sets to take advantage of new marketplace niches and new requirements for skills. For example, we've already seen this with a wide cross-section of people retraining to be life-coaches, a job that didn't really exist in its modern form 15 years ago. Looking at the IT industry, there was a mad scramble for programmers 20 years ago and anyone who knew more than the basic techniques tended to be hired promptly and given a generous salary. People then moved across to be network specialists, and with the advent of cloud-based data storage, the next change will be to switch to being data analysts.

Trend hopping is a smart way to stay ahead of the game and if we keep abreast of new technology and trends and always have funds available to pay for our own development, we can hop to a new career that abuts our existing one. Two good trend-hopping questions are:

- What is the next big skill-trend in your current industry?
- Where would you like to hop to?

ADDING VALUE IS ESSENTIAL

Thanks to smartphones and in-vehicle monitoring systems, our whereabouts can be tracked and our output can be monitored. We already have corporate computer systems that log our activity and note when our laptop is switched off. Aside from encouraging electronic 'presenteeism' and creative workarounds, it also means that we will stay hired if we add value and lose our jobs if we don't. The ability to hide in a back office for 40 years will be redundant and each day we will be forced to confront our output from the day before and ask: 'Was that good enough?'

This is already the case for many of the growing band of self-employed people who know that they're only as good as their last customer visit and they won't get paid if they don't deliver what the customer wants. Take a moment to think about:

- How much value do you really add?
- What do you need to do more of?

INCREASED OPPORTUNITIES FOR PORTFOLIO WORKING

As a result of the increase in the added-value approach, organisations will realise that they don't need to have us on the payroll for five days a week. Once you subtract periods of inactivity, conversation, travel and waiting time, we only tend to add value for around five or six hours a day, out of a standard 9-to-5 working day. This means that we often need some of the people for all of the time and all of the people for some of the time, but not all of the people for all of the time.

Once we have identified who these people are, we can put them on a three-day per week contract and let them find other work to make up the balance. It also means employers are more open to people working in job-share arrangements or simply working across several different jobs during a week.

Examples of this include a partner in a legal firm who worked a job-share after maternity leave and an office manager who asked to move to a four-day week so that she could retrain and be a hair stylist one day a week. She wanted to have a variety of work and that combination was more fulfilling for her than just being in an office.

Given the increased opportunities for creativity with how we construct and manage our portfolio of jobs, we can ask for what we need and design our lives to suit our preferences. When you think about the possibilities for a portfolio lifestyle:

- How would you like to organise your week?
- What could a portfolio look like for you?

MICRO-JOBS

This concept was used widely in Germany after the 2008/2009 recession, where people were able to work small fixed-hour contracts in return for reduced tax rates. Although this can affect employee benefit packages and raises issues about paid leave, health care provision and pastoral support, it does mean the labour market will become more responsive. This could become an important issue for Group M workers who are more prone to high street trends and demand spikes and therefore more susceptible to having to take short-term or limited-hours contracts. If micro-jobs sound like the future for you:

- How would you manage a basket of micro-jobs?
- How could a micro-job boost your current income?

THE HOME-WORK CAPSULE

We only have to think back to our grandparents' time to realise that houses have changed dramatically in the last 70 years and now generally all have electric lighting, central heating and, best of all, a bathroom and toilet within the house. With the increasing trend for people to work at home for part of the week and to be able to telecommute using video software and email, it might well be essential to have a discrete work suite tucked away in a corner. This could contain superfast next-generation broadband, a glass wall for video sharing and the projection of data for synchronised discussions and a 3-D printer, which will produce anything we need on demand.

What this means for us is that we will continue to have

to pay close attention to our internet access when choosing where to live and make sure that we have a 'professional space' to work in. Given that internet access is already becoming a differentiator of earning potential:

- What do you need to consider with regards to internet connectivity?
- What do you need to invest in?

CLOUD + 3-D

The use of cloud storage facilities to hold vast amounts of data in easily accessible, yet entirely remote, locations frees up organisations from having local data centres and from having to co-locate the necessary support or operational staff. They can create 'cloud offices' that may host several hundred people, all of whom are not physically present in the same space and may be drawn from across several language zones.

The 3-D printer will be a thing of marvel, to rival the advent of the magic cooking machine (the microwave) and the magic recording machine (the video cassette recorder). Whether we use ours to print toys, birthday cards or a new sofa is yet to be decided, however we can be sure that it will do for the postal service what internet shopping did for mass market high street retailers.

With a 3-D printer, engineers can print complex components on demand and thus work anywhere in the world. Retailers can sell 'patterns' and remove the need for packaging and transportation. Once we can print off a pizza (it's coming soon to a 3-D printed plate near you), supermarkets may turn into virtual spaces, without the need for Group M employees. When considering technical innovations:

- What products or services do you need to be an early adopter of, to remain at the cutting edge of your career specialisation?
- What changes are you hoping will go away?

VIDEO INTERVIEWS

These are quickly becoming a standard feature of recruitment processes as they are time efficient and allow businesses to search a much wider geographic area for potential candidates. It also means that in the same way middle managers had to learn PowerPoint presentation skills, we will now need to acquire video skills in order to maintain eye contact and communicate more effectively. It also means that using Skype-type packages from our kitchen table will become less feasible, as we'll need to present a clean and professional picture and not have kitchen cupboards and children's artwork as a backdrop. This is where our work-capsule becomes necessary. The uptake of video applications for business is increasing, so:

- Is your home office environment good enough for a video interview session?
- What video skills do you need to practice?

THE CV STAYS

The demise of paper has long been written (electronically), but has yet to come to pass. However, even if we do get used to low intensity easy-read computer screens, the need for a career resumé is here to stay. It will be subject to greater electronic scrutiny, though, through the rise of job-search apps and sites.

While useful websites such as LinkedIn (some people feel that if you're not on it, you don't exist) currently allow us to add searchable career-related information about ourselves, our CV and cover letter – even if delivered by email with a hyperlink back to our personal website, is still a piece of work that *we* have had to do, instead of someone else's form that we filled in.

Hiring people is about connecting with the *right* people and although the use of smartphones, tablet computers and technology for recruitment purposes will be second nature within the next few years, we will still need evidence of our employment history and ability. Perhaps though, the Electro-CV of 2050 will have embedded auto-recorded, high-definition videos of our workplace highlights, ready to play back and impress a recruiter. Take a fresh look at your CV:

- How relevant and value-adding is your CV right now?
- Does it contain key career words to stand out in internet searches and automatic sorting tools?

SOCIAL MEDIA BRAND

The *soc-med* revolution is here to stay and we need to embrace it and make sure that we have a presence on the major platforms, which are currently Facebook, LinkedIn and Twitter. All of them can be used for career management purposes and we can certainly ride the rocket along the connections and networks we belong to in order to research new opportunities, make new friends, increase our sector expertise and introduce ourselves to the world.

Of course, we can also use it to ruin our chances of employment by confusing people about our brand – are we funny on Twitter, serious on LinkedIn and a party animal on Facebook? As more people join the revolution, there will be greater tolerance of us having both a public career persona and a private leisure persona and as long as our values, attitudes and behaviour fall within acceptable norms we will be fine. We need to be coherent across all of the public domains we use – problems will occur if the behaviours conflict or seriously undermine each other. People are naturally conservative and tend to think worse of us if they don't get the joke or fail to grasp the point we're making. When you think about your current use of key public domains:

- What impression do people get from your social media branding?
- What do you need to be more careful about?

INTERNET FOOTPRINT

If our current image is coherent, what is our overall internet footprint? The trend is for people to be published on the internet, often in the form of guest blogs, articles or tagged photographs. We also need to make sure old website entries and party photographs are removed if they are now out of date or unhelpful to our current position. Given that the golden rule for the internet is *once it's been posted it's there forever,* we do need to be cautious about the footprint we are creating for ourselves. Although people may forgive youthful indiscretions, employers are increasingly making global searches of job candidates' internet presence as a way of finding out more about them during their decision-making process.

We need to Google ourselves and make sure our internet footprint is the size and shape we need it to be. Think about your footprint and consider these questions:

- Is your internet presence helpful to your modern career?
- What needs to be cleaned up?

BECOME GENERATION AWARE

Given that we will be riding the rocket for more years than our predecessors, up to our delayed retirement, we will meet and work with more people from across the generations. This means that we need to become *generation aware* and acknowledge their differences, tolerate them and work with them. The key generations that are currently defined include:

- Baby Boomers (born 1945 to 1960) – no computers in school.
- Generation X (born 1960 to 1980) – one 'sacred' computer locked away for safety.
- Generation Y (born 1980 to 2000) – a room of computers at school, known as an IT lab.
- Generation Z (born 2000 to 2013) – a computer in their bedroom and in their pocket.[17]

---

[17] Reference: www.wikipedia.com and related searches. There is some debate about the actual years, so I've rounded them up for clarity.

I've used the increased presence of computers in our early years of education as the defining characteristic of each generation, because it tends to set the tone for our acceptance of and confidence with technology. Generation Y, often referred to as *Millenials*, have a high degree of confidence with technology and are less interested in formality and hierarchy than Baby Boomers tend to be. If we're a Millennial then we're more likely to want to wear casual clothes to work and keep our headphones on when working independently. This has no relation to our output – we just like to be comfortable at work. Generation Z are the connected kids who have no knowledge of a world without laptops and smartphones. Often referred to as *Digital Natives*, they see technology as an enabler and don't have to think twice about embracing a new system that offers benefits to them, or a new app or craze that amuses them. Millenials and Digital Natives have grown up in a freer technological environment are thus more interested in collaborating and sharing ideas and information.

Crucially, many of them have also grown up watching their parents' jobs get made redundant and seeing first-hand how unreliable and cruel corporate working life can be. They've witnessed the demise of the traditional career and are now riding their rockets through their modern careers.

It doesn't matter what generation we belong to – what matters is that our attitude towards our colleagues and contemporaries is one of inclusion and thoughtfulness. This way, we forge new networks and adapt to the world around us, instead of wasting our energy grumbling that 'it wasn't like that in our day'. Being generation aware enables us to build rapport with people of all ages, so:

- What can you learn from other generations?
- What do you need to be more tolerant of?

SO WHAT?

Trends are important. If we ignore them we greatly increase the risk of being left behind or of wasting time, or we leave it too late to change the shape and size of our business in response to market dynamics. Over the last couple of years I've worked with a range of clients across the world using Skype as a coaching medium and that's enabled me to reduce travel costs, increase added-value time and be more responsive. I've cut my driving from 30,000 miles a year to 15,000 miles – and who wouldn't want to do that?

I'm not being smug here, because I can still remember being incredulous two years ago when a potential client said to use Skype, instead of me driving a six-hour round trip to see her for 30 minutes. I was concerned – would she really be convinced by a simple video call? Surely face-to-face has that added personal touch we lose through a screen? Well, the answer was that she was convinced and became a client and instead of six hours in my car, I spent the rest of the day outside in the sunshine. We can all learn to follow a trend.

Social media does remind us of the benefit of being social –

we get to interact with clients and colleagues throughout the day and not just for the hour we're in the meeting with them, which enables us to maintain and deepen critical relationships. However, if we allow ourselves to get distracted by our need to stay on top of emails and Tweets, we can easily find ourselves working an 18-hour day from the second we wake up to the second before we go to sleep. Perhaps that's one trend we do need to avoid?

LEARNING EXERCISE

This chapter has included a heady mix of technology, marketplace and people-related trends. You are free to disagree with the expert panel and write in your trends here. Or, you could re-read this chapter and pick out:

A) One trend that is relevant to you now:

_____

_____

B) One trend that you need to watch closely over the next 12 months:

_____

_____

12
Longevity
– Waving Goodbye –

COCKPIT QUESTION:
How healthy will you be in ten years' time?

TIME IS INESCAPABLE

Each of us will reach the day when it's time to throttle back, put down the landing skids and bring our rocket back to the hanger and park it one last time. Our career is over and we can let go of the control column, switch off the boosters, the navigation systems and our radar sweepers. We've ridden the rocket, found destinations that engaged us, have remained in awareness, accelerated up and over to new roles, avoided career killers and learnt about our core skills, embraced the next generation of colleagues and remained enthusiastic about technology along the way.

We have been a success and can now go and do something else.

TO RETIRE OR NOT TO RETIRE – THAT IS THE QUESTION

We are all being asked to work for longer and the coveted position of retiring at 60 years old for women and 65 years old for men has now been forgotten. We can now only retire when (and if) we can afford to, or when we lose the ability to do our job and have to admit defeat.

How we define 'retirement' is up to us and it doesn't mean necessarily having to stop work completely – perhaps we can take a less stressful job, turn a hobby into a small business or collaborate with a friend to set up a service business.

We need to plan for retirement and even though the thought of reaching 70 years old and calling it a day may seem a long way off, we *will* eventually get there. It will help us to be prepared and not be surprised that the last 40 years just vanished in a blip!

USE IT OR LOSE IT

There is a growing body of evidence that continuing to work into older age helps to stave off the onset of dementia by keeping our brain active. It could be well worth considering a second or third career to take us past our 60s and into our 70s because it can contribute to better mental health, by reducing the onset of afflictions such as Alzheimer's disease.

In 2009, researchers at King's College London published a survey which looked at 1,320 dementia patients that included 382 men. They found that for the males in the survey who had continued to work later in life, their active lifestyle had reduced the onset of dementia by helping to keep their brain active and their neurons firing.[18]

Dementia is caused by a mass loss of brain cells and to counteract this, we can spend time stimulating our brain with new things to learn and new problems to solve. We need to think of the brain as a muscle that needs proper exercise, and not as a lump of putty that swims aimlessly between our ears.

If we have been off work for an extended period, our life can quickly reduce in scope and complexity. Where we once thought nothing of catching a flight to the USA, we could now think that walking to the shops is a big deal.

And so it is with our brain – if we want to keep working at any level we need to build up what experts call a 'cognitive reserve' in the same way that athletes add muscle to give them spring and speed and agility. Consider your own grey matter:

- If you visualise your brain now what would it look like? A champion hurdler or a slouched couch potato?

HOW TO RETIRE AND STAY ALIVE

While this header may sound grim, there is evidence that people who lead a hectic working life involving 60 hours a week of coffee, stress, travel, more coffee and more stress have a tendency to fall apart when they suddenly stop. This may come in the form of a heart attack, which is an unpleasant way to end your working life before you've had a chance to cash in your pension and head off into the sunset as aged and heavily-wrinkled backpacker.

Most of us will have developed a cold or a cough on the

[18]   Reference: 'Keep Working to Avoid Dementia' – www.news.bbc.co.uk (May 2009)

second day of a holiday, despite being fine the week before. Our ability to soak up germs and keep working is legendary – until we stop and all the bugs spring into action as we calm down and try to repair the damage our working life has caused.

Therefore, if we want to retire and stay alive we need to avoid the cliff edge that takes us from 100mph of work, stress and excitement to freefall and a dead stop. We need to have a gentle transition from full-on work to full-on retirement, so that our bodies can decelerate smoothly and cope with the change in our environment and in our stress levels.

CASE STUDY – MITCH

Mitch didn't really want to retire because the office was full of his friends and memories. As the final year of his employment loomed into view, his manager suggested he work a 'retirement year' that began with 5 days a week of service and gradually reduced to 1 day a week and then stopped. Mitch didn't like the sound of that as he would be earning less, but his manager assured him he would be on full pay and benefits for the whole year. The purpose of the exercise was not to steal money from him under the guise of being generous with time, but instead to allow him a chance to develop outside interests and to give his wife the chance to adjust to his retirement as well.

It turned out that Mitch had one of the happiest years of his working life and spent his days sorting out his shed, buying new wood-working tools and beginning little projects to make shelves and gift boxes and so on. Towards the end of his year, Mitch's manager noticed that he was unhappy at work and asked why:

'Well now,' said Mitch, 'I've got so many wood-working projects that I really don't have time to come to work anymore and it's getting in the way! I used to dread the thought of retirement and now I have to drag myself in to work!'

And then they both laughed at the realisation of what he had said and how by having a graduated retirement plan, Mitch had been able to safely make the transition from full-time office worker to full-time carpenter.

He had avoided the cliff edge and the prospect of a stress-related heart attack and was instead poised for a long and productive retirement.

SO WHAT?

Health is wealth. Without it, we won't have the option to ride our rocket and if our career is going to spin into our 7th decade, we need to be physically and mentally capable of delivering value to others.

Mental alertness is vital to our healthy old age, however we choose to spend it. The next time we go for a run, we can head to the corner shop and buy a book of crossword puzzles for after we've run home. Our legs will be tired, but our brain still needs something to do!

We can plan ahead and can look after our rocket, so that we can keep riding it into our old age. Even if our eyesight and our hearing have faded a bit, our physis is still there for us and we can enjoy being a productive and valued member of our industry, or we can seize the opportunity to make yet another career change. It's our life and our choice.

LEARNING EXERCISE

We can make a commitment to ourselves to remain healthy and to stimulate our brains. We can also think ahead and plan a smooth transition from full-time working life to full- or part-time retirement.

1) How will you continue to stimulate your brain when you're over 60?

_____

_____

2) Please take time to think about your transition into retirement and write down your thoughts below:

_____

_____

13
Take the Controls
– Put The Learning Into Practice –

COCKPIT QUESTION:
What is the most important personal development point that
you're taking away with you?

YOUR TURN NOW

Throughout this book, we have explored the essentials of
modern career management so we can ride our rocket and have
a great working life. The chapters are full of tips and models,
ideas to follow and new vocabulary to prick our awareness.

It's now time for us to put the book down and put these
things into practice – we need to focus on riding our rocket and
in doing so take control of our direction, our height and our
speed and create opportunities for ourselves.

We are riding our rocket – we are in charge and it's up to us
to make our modern career what we want it to be.

THANK YOU

It's a pleasure to share experiences and ideas with you and I sincerely wish you a fantastic modern career and that you really get from it what you need – and if you ever find yourself stuck, you can always re-read this book and make changes.

Well done!
You've read the book and are all set to ride the rocket of your modern career!

Have a great time and enjoy the flight!
Good wishes to you!

Richard Maun
Norfolk
England
2013

14
Toolkit
– One Life, One Rocket –

This chapter contains a summary of the key tools and models, ideas and career tips from the preceding chapters. It is designed to be a quick reference guide for people in a hurry, or who are stuck and need a prompt to help their thinking and decision making.

1. CAREERS COUNT
– Riding Our Rocket –

A CAREER… is how we spend our time between starting work and retiring.

A CAREER… encompasses our dreams and our ambitions and the things we do to make them a reality.

A CAREER… is the content of our earned life and includes all periods of work, job hunting and vocational training and development.

RICHARD'S 'BE UNCOMMON' GROUP CLASSIFICATION

GROUP A IGNORERS	GROUP B LEAVERS	GROUP C DISMISSERS	GROUP D ACCEPTERS	GROUP E CHOOSERS
Those who don't buy career books, because they're dull.	Those who buy career books because they feel it's the right thing to do, but then leave them on the shelf to sweat their way into their brain.	Those who actually read the books they buy, but tend to cough and crow that they're full of common sense and add little value	Those who are big enough to realise that such books do contain genuinely useful ideas to support increased success.	Those who buy the books, read the books, choose ideas and tools that appeal to them and then actually put them into practice.
No progress is made	No progress is made	No progress is made	Some progress is made	Reasonable, sustained progress is made. If you're here then you're really uncommon and can celebrate!

2. THE CAREER ENGINE
– Keeping Us In Flight –

THE CAREER ENGINE

CAREER TOP TIP

*The more autonomy we have over our working day,
the less stressed we tend to be.*

We can prize autonomy and the flexibility to choose as
two of the most important facets of a successful and
happy modern career.

ALWAYS ASK:
What's the opportunity?

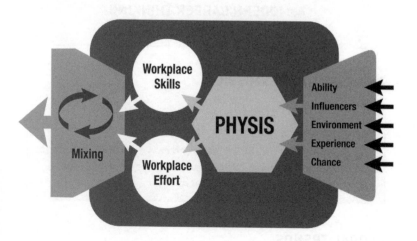

---

3. FRAMING OUR CAREER
– *Progress To Date* –

RICHARD'S REFLECTION ON THE NATURE OF CAREERS:

A. I'm the common denominator.

B. I'm a good person with skill and talent.

C. It can take a few false starts to find out about yourself and what you like and what you're good at.

D. You have to listen to people.

E. It is possible to change course.

F. Loving what you do matters.

G. That it will turn out alright in the end.

---

4. MODERN CAREER THINKING
– *Key Skills For Success* –

AN ESSENTIAL PERMISSION

This is a truth:

The responsibility for our modern career is ours and ours alone. Therefore, we have permission to manage our lives for our benefit.

GLOBAL TRENDS

Global trends and cultural shifts matter. In today's world, these are the new words that are shaping our culture and our economies:

TRENDS THAT MATTER
- Globalisation
- Collaboration
- Social Media
- Flexibility
- Renewable Energy
- Personal Responsibility

TAKE ME HOME TABLE – THE ESSENTIAL GUIDE TO A SUCCESSFUL MODERN CAREER

7 TENETS OF A MODERN CAREER			
1. Knowing our own competencies	2. Having great job hunting skills	3. Being able to retrain	4. Being able to work in a variety of ways
5. Being responsible for our money management		6. Not knowing where our career will be when we retire	7. Not knowing when retirement will be
MODERN CAREER SKILLS			
External Skills 1. Productivity 2. People Skills 3. Public Relations These multiply to give us our *Organisational Impact Score*, which is a useful measure of added value.		**Internal Skills** 1. Agility 2. Determination 3. Humility 4. Learning 5. Reliability 6. Resilience 7. Thinking	**Specialist Skills** 1. Technical language 2. Trade skills 3. Process skills
6 CAREER CHALLENGES			
1. To do the job we're paid for		2. To keep developing	3. To maintain our energy
4. To remain open minded		5. To think forwards	6. To be true to ourselves

---

ORGANISATIONAL IMPACT SCORE

Use the sum to find your score

Productivity self-score out of 20
x
People skills self-score out of 15
x
Public relations self-score out of 10

= ?/20 x ?/15 x ?/10

=_____

Your total score divided by 3,000

For example, your scores might be as follows: 10 x 8 x 5 = 400 ÷ 3,000 = 0.133.

Our score then places us in one of three zones. Where are you?

1. **Keeper Zone.** If we score between 1.000 and 0.420 then we're in the high performing *Keeper Zone* and are doing a great job.

2. **Cruiser Zone.** If we score between 0.420 and 0.040 then we're in the *Cruiser Zone*, where the majority of people spend most of their working lives.

3. **Cutter Zone.** If we score between 0.040 and 0.000 then we are in the *Cutter Zone*, which means we have one foot outside the door, or need to seek immediate support.

5. AWARENESS PLEASE
– Don't Be A Tourist –

THE ENEMIES OF AWARENESS INCLUDE:
- Fatigue
- Fear
- Stress
- Inexperience
- Lack of Interest
- Filtering

6. HOW TO CHOOSE CAREERS
– Navigation Lessons –

CAREER TOP TIP

Trust your intuition!
(It knows you better than you do.)

ACCESSING INTUITION

Q1) What areas of work do you feel drawn to?
Q2) Who do you secretly admire and wish you had their job?
Q3) Which jobs leave you feeling cold when someone suggests them to you?
Q4) What roles do you find yourself researching over and over again?

JOB GRID

Stylist	Mentor	Commander	Writer	Farmer	Postman	Nurse	Programmer	Engineer	Researcher
Hotelier	Policeman	Potter	Buyer	Lawyer	Entrepreneur	Priest	Athlete	Footballer	Cook
Chef	Paramedic	Healer	Planner	Historian	Salesperson	Adventurer	Campaigner	Social Worker	Assembler
Creator	Tailor	Teacher	Dancer	Sailor	Agent	Coach	Designer	Pilot	Vet
Editor	Architect	Musician	Cargiver	Photographer	Linguist	Waiter	Firefighter	Carpenter	Traveller
Inventor	Consultant	Zookeeper	Rescuer	Administrator	Plumber	Politician	Cleaner	Director	Painter
Artist	Fitness Instructor	Doctor	Shop Assistant	Supervisor	Journalist	Networker	Celebrity	Officer	Fisherman
Comedian	Scholar	Daredevil	Actor	Critic	Receptionist	Soldier	Scientist	Host	Producer
Trader	Promoter	Youth Worker	Driver	Accountant	Operative	Lecturer	Owner	Singer	Model
Advisor	Marketer	Curator	Clerk	Sculptor	Mechanic	Supervisor	Designer	Builder	

SKILLS & ATTRIBUTES GRID

Prefers exercise to sitting	Proactive	Exudes warmth	Accepts direction	Works well alone	Enjoys competition	Organised	Authoritative	Reads maps	Politically astute
Enjoys new things	Ambitious	Public speaking	Collaborates	Walking	Facility for language	Thinks deeply	Witty	Caring for others	Follows rules
Assertive	Notices Others	Punctual	Finds out information	Can see patterns	Intuitive	Diligent	Calm	Dedicated	Takes measured risks
Reliable	Team player	Animal husbandry	Creative	Neat and tidy	Complex mathematics	Polite	Plans thoroughly	Embraces change	Is listened to
Good in a crisis	Working with hands	Likes the outdoors	Good at learning	Seeks challenges	Patient	Problem solver	Talking	Practical	Can remember theories
Resourceful	Engages people	Playful	Reading	Sells ideas	Strong sense of spatial awareness	Writing	Inventive	Reactive	Careful
Enjoys detail	Can draw	Confident with arithmetic	Presenting	Builds consensus	Can follow orders	Always completes tasks	Analysis and deduction	Listens	Accepts other points of view
Good at fixing things	Leads from the front	Explores	Creates solutions	Smiles	Has a flexible outlook	Independent	Works at speed	Works well under pressure	Lively

Career Dynamics Exercise – On each line, put a cross closest to the box that best fits your career/role preferences.

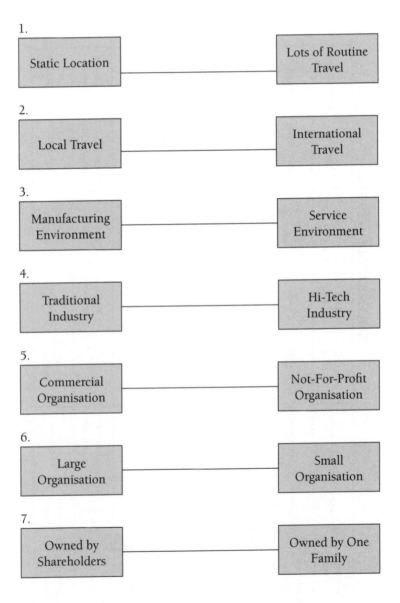

1.

| Static Location | Lots of Routine Travel |

2.

| Local Travel | International Travel |

3.

| Manufacturing Environment | Service Environment |

4.

| Traditional Industry | Hi-Tech Industry |

5.

| Commercial Organisation | Not-For-Profit Organisation |

6.

| Large Organisation | Small Organisation |

7.

| Owned by Shareholders | Owned by One Family |

8.

| Fast-paced Environment | —— | Slower-paced Environment |

9.

| Rapidly-Changing Environment | —— | Static Environment |

10.

| Promotion Through Time Served | —— | Promotion by Ability |

11.

| High Freedom to Act | —— | Follow Set Procedures |

12.

| Work with People | —— | Work with Tasks |

13.

| Detailed, Careful Work | —— | Simpler, General Tasks |

14.

| Full Time | —— | Part Time |

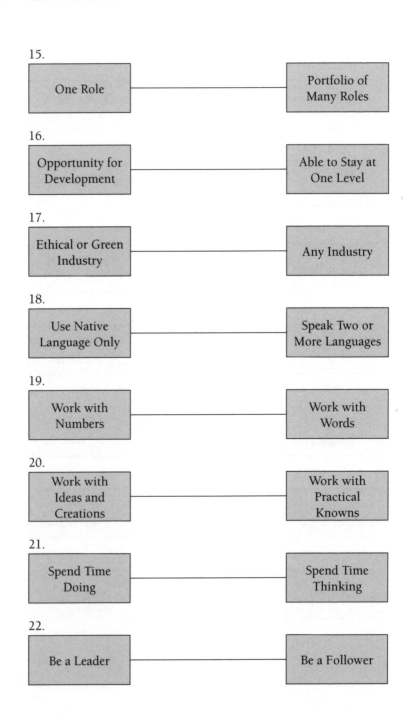

15.

| One Role | Portfolio of Many Roles |

16.

| Opportunity for Development | Able to Stay at One Level |

17.

| Ethical or Green Industry | Any Industry |

18.

| Use Native Language Only | Speak Two or More Languages |

19.

| Work with Numbers | Work with Words |

20.

| Work with Ideas and Creations | Work with Practical Knowns |

21.

| Spend Time Doing | Spend Time Thinking |

22.

| Be a Leader | Be a Follower |

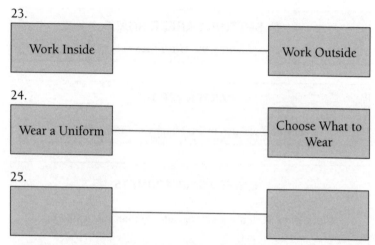

23.

Work Inside ——————— Work Outside

24.

Wear a Uniform ——————— Choose What to Wear

25.

Your choice – please add your own dynamic here.

IF you want it – you can have it

AND you've got to be prepared to pay for it…!!!

7. SETTING CAREER GOALS
– Money vs. Happiness –

CAREER TOP TIP

The best place to be is… happy in the middle.

CAREER GOAL PROMPTS

Which ones fit and which ones are you not interested in?

Obtain a university degree.
Secure the top job in your field.
Own your own business.
Become financially independent.
Acquire a specific expertise.
Become known as a world expert.
Campaign for change.
Win a specific award.
Leave your mark on the world.
Work for the good of society.
Found an organisation.
Publish or record something.
Be awarded a medal.
Be happy in the middle.

8. HOW TO CHANGE CAREERS
– *Pulling G* –

The model invites us to think about the degree of complexity associated with the career change that we wish to make.

CAREER TOP TIP

Reduce risk by changing one thing at a time.

For example, if we want to go from being a doctor's receptionist to a hotel manager, it would make sense to move across to the right industry as a hotel receptionist first, before moving up the management ranks to the right job.

4 STEPS OF SUCCESSFUL NETWORKING
Meet – Ask – Connect – Ask

1. **Meet People Face to Face.** Although I'm a big fan of social media, there is still a place for meeting face to face, where we can smile, shake hands and size each other up.
2. **Ask Questions.** If we want to get to know people then we need to ask them questions to get them talking and then *listen* to the answers.
3. **Connecting counts.** If networking is a secret of success then connecting with people is the secret within the secret.
4. **Ask for Something.** It's okay for us to want things and to be ambitious.

9. CAREER ACCELERATORS
– Flying Higher, Flying Faster –

SECTION 1) PEOPLE SKILLS

1.1 Easy To Do Business With

1.2 Engaging With People

1.3 Being Present

1.4 Being Visible

1.5 Building The Psychological

1.6 Medal Days

SECTION 2) TECHNICAL SKILLS

2.1 Generating Good News

2.2 Being Brilliant

2.3 Networking

2.4 Education

2.5 Adding Value & Removing Waste

There are eight different types of waste to look out for and they are:

1. Overproduction

2. Waiting

3. Transporting

4. Inappropriate Processing

5. Unnecessary Inventory

6. Unnecessary Movement

7. Defects

8. People

CAREER TOP TIP

How to remove waste:
1. **Stand still.** Observe people at work.
2. **Look for piles of paper work.** These tell us when people are working hard and are under-resourced.
3. **Walk the process.** This is a great way to make the invisible come to life.
4. **Mine our frustrations.** We often know what is causing us to waste time and effort.

10. THE CAREER KILLERS
– Becoming Toxic –

THE CAREER KILLERS MODEL

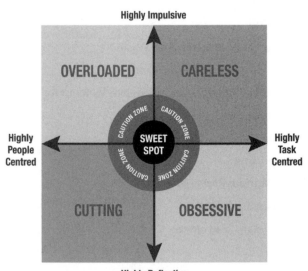

11. AN ESSENTIAL GUIDE TO CAREER TRENDS
– Preparing For The Future –

NOBODY IS FUTURE-PROOF

It's tempting to argue that there are some careers which are immune to the vagaries of changing technological, sociological and geographical trends, but that's a myth.

GROUP P AND GROUP M

The working world will become more sharply divided between people who have professional level skills (Group P) and those who have other more menial skills (Group M).

NOMADS AND SILOS

Given the requirement for organisations to be agile and only hire skills when needed, there will tend to be a greater number of nomadic self-employed people and single-handed consultancies. Increased specialisation in organisations will create more departmental silos.

TREND HOPPING

We will increasingly move between skill sets to take advantage of new marketplace niches and new requirements for skills.

ADDING VALUE IS ESSENTIAL

The ability to hide in a back office for 40 years will be lost and each day we will be forced to confront our output from the day before and ask: 'Was that good enough?'

INCREASED OPPORTUNITIES FOR PORTFOLIO WORKING

As a result of the increase in the added value approach, organisations will realise they don't need to have us on the payroll for five days a week.

MICRO-JOBS

This concept was used widely in Germany, after the 2008/2009 recession, where people were able to work small fixed-hour contracts in return for reduced tax rates.

THE HOME-WORK CAPSULE

This will contain superfast next-generation broadband, a glass wall for video sharing and the instant projection of data for synchronised discussions and a 3-D printer, which will produce anything we need on demand.

CLOUD + 3-D

The use of cloud storage facilities to hold vast amounts of data in easily accessible, yet entirely remote, locations frees up organisations from having local data centres and from having to co-locate the necessary support or operational staff. 3-D printers will be commonplace and change the way goods are delivered – straight to our desks.

VIDEO INTERVIEWS

These are quickly becoming a standard feature of recruitment processes as they are time efficient and allow businesses to search a much wider geographic area for potential candidates.

THE CV STAYS

The need for a career resumé will remain. It will be subject to greater electronic scrutiny, though, through the rise of job-search apps and sites.

SOCIAL MEDIA BRAND

The *soc-med* revolution is here to stay and we need to embrace it and make sure that we have a presence on the major platforms, which are currently Facebook, LinkedIn and Twitter.

INTERNET FOOTPRINT

What is our overall internet footprint? Do we need to clean up our footprint and delete content?

BECOME GENERATION AWARE

We need to collaborate with colleagues from all generations. The key generations that are currently defined include:

- Baby Boomers (born 1945 to 1960) – no computers in school.
- Generation X (born 1960 to 1980) – one 'sacred' computer locked away for safety.
- Generation Y (born 1980 to 2000) – a room of computers at school, known as an IT lab.
- Generation Z (born 2000 to 2013) – a computer in their bedroom and in their pocket.

12. LONGEVITY
– Waving Goodbye –

USE IT OR LOSE IT

There is a growing body of evidence that continuing to work into older age helps to stave off the onset of dementia by keeping our brain active. If we want to retire and stay alive we need to avoid the cliff edge that takes us from 100mph of work, stress and excitement to freefall and a dead stop. We need to have a gentle transition from full-on work to full-on retirement, so that our bodies can decelerate smoothly and cope with the change in our environment and our stress levels.

Remember: Health is Wealth

13. TAKE THE CONTROLS
– Put The Learning Into Practice –

YOUR TURN NOW

You are riding your rocket – you are in charge and it's up to you to make your modern career what you want it to be.

Go for it!

Preview of *Building the Rocket*

– Companion Mini E-book –

Building the Rocket is an e-book only mini companion volume to *Riding the Rocket*. It's been written as a bite-sized career book, designed to promote thinking and to be read during a coffee break. The book contains unique content and a preview of *Riding the Rocket*.

Contents:

- **Welcome to the Workshop** – How to build our rocket, so that we can fly it and enjoy a successful working life.
- **Modern careers** – the path we all travel along.
- **Success Factors** – What three attributes do people need to have in order to create a successful career for themselves?
- **Is This You?** – In the world of work, career, life and general struggle, there are two groups of people. Those who make things easy for themselves and those who don't. Which of the two groups do you fall into?
- **10 Essential Foundations** – Ten strengthening bolts to be included in the construction of our rocket.
- **Enjoy the Ride** – We can all build our rocket and then fly it well. We can take care of ourselves, we can make choices that work for us and we can enjoy the ride!

Building the Rocket by Richard Maun is available online from leading e-book stores.

Introducing Other Richard Maun Books from Marshall Cavendish

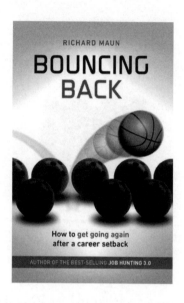

We live in times of global recession and slow recovery, where millions of people are facing redundancy, failed businesses, or the effects of cutbacks and budget reductions. *Bouncing Back* is for anyone who has suffered a setback in their career, who wants to make sense of the new world, and who wants to recover and move on quickly.

In order to bounce back, we need to develop resilience and agility so we can see the world as a place of opportunity rather than limitation. Resilience is about coming to terms with ourselves and creating the energy to keep us motivated. Agility involves having a good set of thinking skills, talking with new people and being able to let go of what isn't working and choose new directions. This practical and inspiring book offers essential skills for surviving and overcoming the disruptions in your career. It could even lead you onto a new and more fulfilling career path!

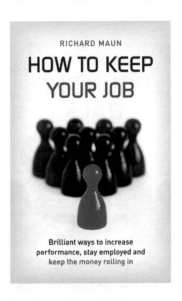

If you have a job, would you like to keep it? In these difficult and unstable times, the answer is most likely to be a resounding YES!

This book reveals the secrets of keeping your job. It cuts to the heart of modern working life and examines the big things that trip people up and what you need to know in order to survive – because you need more than just technical skills to stay employed. You need to know how to become an added value employee.

Based on first-hand experiences of coaching people to keep their job, packed with practical tips and simple to apply, the content is designed to enable people to excel in their workplace.

How To Keep Your Job is an easy-to-read, highly practical manual for success that every modern worker needs to have if they want to reduce their stress, increase their skills and add more value, in order to stay employed and keep the money rolling in!

The secrets and skills contained in this book can make a life-changing difference to your job hunting activities, because they are based on real-world experience and have been used by real people to get real jobs.

Packed with practical tips, essential tools, detailed examples and revealing the three big secrets of success, *Job Hunting 3.0* can accelerate you past the rest of your competitors and into a winning position.

To be successful in the modern world we need to know how to package our talents, how to unearth opportunities and how to assert ourselves when it matters. We need to be able to build rapport with people, talk fluently about how we can add value and be agile with our thinking in order to maximise our core strengths. We also need to use technology to our advantage and embrace the new wave of social media opportunities. Moreover, *Job Hunting 3.0* is built on process thinking, because job hunting is a sales *process* and if you set up and follow a good process, you will create opportunities for positive outcomes.

In this book you will learn about the essential elements of job hunting in the modern age, including the three-horse race, the Minute To Win It, the STAR answering technique, the demons model, the 20+ places where you can look for work, performance ratios, using numbers effectively to add value to your CV, killer questions, winning at assessment centres, the pause button, aces high and the 5-slide formula.

Job Hunting 3.0 takes us through all of these elements and more, with one goal in mind: to get you ahead of the competition so that you can secure your next job.

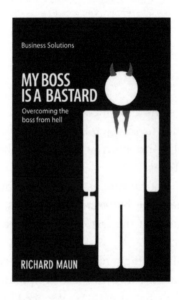

Do you have a reasonable, competent, fair-minded and even-tempered boss? Congratulations! You need read no further.

Still with us? Then you are probably one of the vast majority who have problems with your manager. He or she may be difficult, temperamental, even downright brutal, but for the sake of your career (and your sanity), you have to achieve some kind of working relationship. That's where *My Boss is a Bastard* comes in.

With a compelling blend of insight, wit and candour, Richard Maun dissects the personality types that make bad bosses and offers practical tips to help you survive everyday encounters with the monster in your office. Forewarned is forearmed: once you have recognised the raw animal nature that lurks beneath that plausible professional exterior – is it lion? Elephant? Crocodile? Or even meerkat? – you'll be better equipped to escape unscathed from your next brush with the boss. That way, you can make sure that you don't inflict on others the miseries you've had inflicted on you.

This book offers a lifeline for anyone suffering from a hostile work environment, and can help you transform the way you communicate and interact with others. It also contains a useful Personal Survival Kit, designed to help you really think about where you are and then take positive steps towards a happier, brighter and bastard-free future.

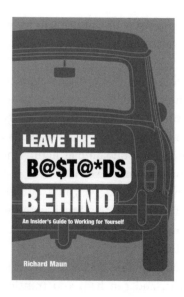

Ever thought of working for yourself? Of course you have – and all the time! This is the book you wish you had ten years ago.

For many people, working for themselves is something that they yearn for and dream about. You've worked for other people's companies and been bossed around by terrible bosses for years. The time has now come to work for the best boss you could have – i.e., yourself.

This book is a straightforward, lively guide to the realities of setting up your own business, written from first-hand experience. Share in the disaster of the author's first sales meeting. Laugh at the attempts to design a business card, and wince at the pace of learning required to stay one step ahead of clients. Through such experiences, the author reveals the secrets of developing a client base and the skills which will help you through the door to self-employment in all its bare-knuckle glory. Working for yourself is one of the richest experiences in life. This practical and inspirational book will put you on the road to success.

About the Author

Richard Maun is an international executive development specialist and careers writer. He facilitates personal and organisational development through coaching, training and management consultancy. He is interested in all points of our modern careers compass and works with organisations and private clients to enable to people to change roles, find work, keep their job, improve leadership skills, achieve promotion, solve problems and develop their business.

Richard now runs his own management development company and is a visiting lecturer to a leading UK university and in his work he uses Transactional Analysis and combines it with Lean thinking. He is also an engaging conference speaker, hosts a weekly business radio show and is a freelance business writer. He has published six books with Marshall Cavendish – *Riding the Rocket, Bouncing Back, How To Keep Your Job, Job Hunting 3.0, My Boss is a Bastard* and *Leave The B@$T@*DS Behind* –

that look at how to manage our modern career, recover from a setback, excel in the workplace, get a job in a competitive world, survive turmoil at work and set oneself up in business.

For coaching, training courses, public speaking and e-publishing, visit **www.richardmaun.com**

Richard can also be contacted via:
Modern Careers Blog: www.richardmaun.com/writing
Facebook Page: Richard Maun – Modern Careers
LinkedIn: Richard Maun
Twitter: @RichardMaun
Skype: richardmaun